YOUR LIFE
IN CHRIST

VICTORYSERIES

STUDY **6**

YOUR LIFE
IN CHRIST

WALK IN FREEDOM
BY FAITH

NEIL T. ANDERSON

BETHANYHOUSE
a division of Baker Publishing Group
www.BethanyHouse.com

Published by Bethany House Publishers
11400 Hampshire Avenue South
Bloomington, Minnesota 55438
www.bethanyhouse.com

Bethany House Publishers is a division of
Baker Publishing Group, Grand Rapids, Michigan

Printed in the United States of America

Library of Congress Control Number: 2014958631

ISBN 978-0-7642-1703-6

Unless otherwise indicated, Scripture quotations are from the Holy Bible, New International Version®. NIV®. Copyright © 1973, 1978, 1984, 2011 by Biblica, Inc.™ Used by permission of Zondervan. All rights reserved worldwide. www.zondervan.com

Scripture quotations identified NASB are from the New American Standard Bible®, copyright © 1960, 1962, 1963, 1968, 1971, 1972, 1973, 1975, 1977, 1995 by The Lockman Foundation. Used by permission.

Cover design by Rob Williams, InsideOutCreativeArts

15 16 17 18 19 20 21   7 6 5 4 3 2 1

Contents

Contents

Introduction

The Victory Series

S o then, just as you received Christ Jesus as Lord, continue to live your lives in him, rooted and built up in him, strengthened in the faith as you were taught" (Colossians 2:6–7). Paul's New Covenant theology is based on who we are "in Christ." As a believer in Christ, you must first be rooted "in Him" so you can be built up "in Him." Just as you encounter challenges as you grow physically, you will encounter hurdles as you grow spiritually. The following chart illustrates what obstacles you need to overcome and lessons you need to learn at various stages of growth spiritually, rationally, emotionally, volitionally, and relationally.

Levels of Conflict

	Level One Rooted in Christ	Level Two Built up in Christ	Level Three Living in Christ
Spiritual	Lack of salvation or assurance (Eph. 2:1–3)	Living according to the flesh (Gal. 5:19–21)	Insensitive to the Spirit's leading (Heb. 5:11–14)
Rational	Pride and ignorance (1 Cor. 8:1)	Wrong belief or philosophy (Col. 2:8)	Lack of knowledge (Hos. 4:6)
Emotional	Fearful, guilty, and shameful (Matt. 10:26–33; Rom. 3:23)	Angry, anxious, and depressed (Eph. 4:31; 1 Pet. 5:7; 2 Cor. 4:1–18)	Discouraged and sorrowful (Gal. 6:9)

	Level One Rooted in Christ	**Level Two** Built up in Christ	**Level Three** Living in Christ
Volitional	Rebellious (1 Tim. 1:9)	Lack of self-control (1 Cor. 3:1–3)	Undisciplined (2 Thess. 3:7, 11)
Relational	Rejected and unloved (1 Pet. 2:4)	Bitter and unforgiving (Col. 3:13)	Selfish (1 Cor. 10:24; Phil. 2:1–5)

This VICTORY SERIES will address these obstacles and hurdles and help you understand what it means to be firmly rooted in Christ, grow in Christ, live free in Christ, and overcome in Christ. The goal of the course is to help you attain greater levels of spiritual growth, as the following diagram illustrates:

Levels of Growth

	Level One Rooted in Christ	**Level Two** Built up in Christ	**Level Three** Living in Christ
Spiritual	Child of God (Rom. 8:16)	Lives according to the Spirit (Gal. 5:22–23)	Led by the Spirit (Rom. 8:14)
Rational	Knows the truth (John 8:32)	Correctly uses the Bible (2 Tim. 2:15)	Adequate and equipped (2 Tim. 3:16–17)
Emotional	Free (Gal. 5:1)	Joyful, peaceful, and patient (Gal. 5:22)	Contented (Phil. 4:11)
Volitional	Submissive (Rom. 13:1–5)	Self-controlled (Gal. 5:23)	Disciplined (1 Tim. 4:7–8)
Relational	Accepted and forgiven (Rom. 5:8; 15:7)	Forgiving (Eph. 4:32)	Loving and unselfish (Phil. 2:1–5)

God's Story for You and *Your New Identity,* the first two studies in the VICTORY SERIES, focused on the issues that help the believer become firmly rooted in Christ (level one in above chart). If you have completed those studies, then you know the whole gospel, who you are in Christ, and who your heavenly Father is. The three subsequent studies—*Your Foundation in Christ, Renewing Your Mind*, and *Growing in Christ*—and this study, *Your Life in Christ,* discuss issues related to your spiritual growth and daily living (levels two and three in the above chart).

As you work through the six sessions in this Bible study, you will discover how to discern God's will and assess whether you are walking in faith according to God's Word. You will learn biblical principles of leadership and how to disciple others and help them find true freedom in Christ from a biblical worldview perspective. "The Steps to Freedom in Christ" will be mentioned during this study. This booklet can be purchased at any Christian bookstore or from Freedom in Christ Ministries. The Steps to Freedom in Christ is a repentance process that can help you resolve your personal and spiritual conflicts. The theology and application of the Steps is explained in the book *Discipleship Counseling*.

Before starting each daily reading, review the portion of Scripture listed for that day, then complete the questions at the end of each day's reading. These questions have been written to allow you to reflect on the material and apply to your life the ideas presented in the reading. At the end of each study, I have included a quote from a Church father illustrating the continuity of the Christian faith. Featured articles will appear in the text throughout the series, which are for the edification of the reader and not necessarily meant for discussion.

If you are part of a small group, be prepared to share your thoughts and insights with your group. You may also want to set up an accountability partnership with someone in your group to encourage you as you apply what you have learned in each session. For those of you who are leading a small group, there are leader tips at the end of this book that will help you guide your participants through the material.

As with any spiritual discipline, you will be tempted at times not to finish this study. There is a "sure reward" for those who make a "sure commitment." The VICTORY SERIES is far more than an intellectual exercise. The truth will not set you free if you only acknowledge it and discuss it on an intellectual level. For the truth to transform your life, you must believe it personally and allow it to sink deep into your heart. Trust the Holy Spirit to lead you into all truth and enable you to be the person God has created you to be. Decide to live what you have chosen to believe.

Dr. Neil T. Anderson

God's Will

The "oil king" is the person on board a ship who is responsible for the distribution of the fuel. The fuel is stored in several watertight compartments and provides ballast for the ship. If there is only one compartment for the fuel and it ruptures, the ship will become unstable and may sink. However, if only one of several compartments ruptures, the ship will be safe. A ship that is low on fuel or other ballast will sit high in the water and be vulnerable in rough weather.

During World War II, six navy destroyers were low on fuel when they encountered a typhoon in the Pacific Ocean. All six were lost. The oil king has to keep the fuel distributed evenly, or the ship will list from one side to the other. If the oil king lets one compartment go dry before switching to another compartment, the engines will stop, the ship will lose power, and it will again be subject to the sea. A ship at sea is stable only when it is under way. The rudder is useless if the ship isn't moving.

The Holy Spirit is our oil king. We have stability when we are filled with the Spirit and sailing in the right direction. He is the wind who has our back. He keeps us in balance so we don't list from one side to the other. When one member of a family or church is battered by the storms of life, other Spirit-filled members will keep the home and church safe.

Daily Readings

1. Reason and Intuition	1 Corinthians 1:20–31
2. Do All to the Glory of God	1 Corinthians 10:23–33
3. Divine Guidance	2 Kings 2:1–25
4. Making Wise Decisions	Proverbs 3:13–24
5. God Guides a Moving Ship	Acts 16:1–10

1

Reason and Intuition

1 Corinthians 1:20–31

Key Point

Truth is both real and right, making wise the simple and empowering those who are zealous for God.

Key Verse

Be strong in the Lord and in his mighty power.

Ephesians 6:10

Comprehending truth incorporates reason and intuition. Sometimes we just know something to be true without any means of objective verification. In the natural world, the left and right hemispheres of the brain illustrate the objective and subjective nature of reality. This has some correlation with the historical tension in Christianity between Western rationalism and Eastern mysticism.

Jesus is the Truth and so is His Word, but the finite mind cannot fully comprehend the truth. The Holy Spirit enables us to know Jesus and His Word so we can be sanctified. In the following diagram, the kingdom of God is depicted above the horizontal line and the natural world below it.

The bell-shaped curve represents how humanity relates to truth, as depicted at the top and center of the curve.

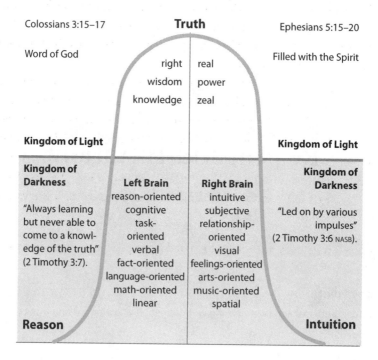

Some people are more naturally intuitive while others are more naturally cognitive. Some are relational and art-oriented, while others are task and math-oriented. The right-brained folks who don't know Jesus are "led on by various impulses" (2 Timothy 3:6 NASB), while the left-brained folks who don't know Jesus are "always learning but never able to come to a knowledge of the truth" (verse 7).

Throughout Scripture, we can see how God balances the two sides. Paul said, "Jews demand signs and Greeks look for wisdom . . . but to those whom God has called, both Jews and Greeks, Christ [is] the power of God and the wisdom of God" (1 Corinthians 1:22, 24). Truth is both real and right, and those who have fully appropriated the truth have zeal and knowledge. We need to let the Word of Christ richly dwell within us (rational), but we also need to be filled with the Spirit (intuitive). Both have the same result (compare Ephesians 5:18–20 with Colossians 3:15–17), and both are required for balance and productivity.

Most western evangelicals lean heavily to the left and emphasize wisdom and knowledge. You could graduate from an evangelical seminary or Bible college because you answered most of the questions correctly. You could do that and be a nonbeliever.

Christians in the West have trouble believing in someone or something they can't fully understand, because they don't have control of what they can't explain. However, Eastern Orthodox Christians don't try to explain what they don't understand. They just say, "It's a mystery." It is easy for Westerners to see the folly of "zeal without knowledge," but they may be less aware that "knowledge puffs up while love builds up" (1 Corinthians 8:1). You can know theology and be arrogant, but you can't know God and be arrogant.

Why do we need both sides of the brain to be complete in our quest for truth?

How does Scripture balance reason and intuition?

What are the dangers of emphasizing either reason or intuition over the other?

Given your church background and your natural bent, how balanced do you think you are right now in your pursuit of Truth? Explain.

_____

_____

_____

Some will say, "It's a mystery," while others will say, "We have to understand this." Which do you think is the right orientation? Why?

_____

_____

_____

To believe in the one who was crucified and buried and to be fully convinced that He rose again does not need more reasoning but faith alone. The apostles themselves were converted not by wisdom but by faith. Once they had that, they surpassed the heathen wise men in both wisdom and intellectual depth. . . . Plato was cast out not by another philosopher of more skill but by unlearned fishers.

John Chrysostom (AD 347–407)

2

Do All to the Glory of God

1 Corinthians 10:23–33

Key Point

The essential prerequisite to knowing the will of God is a willingness to do it before you know what it is.

Key Verse

So whether you eat or drink or whatever you do, do it all for the glory of God.

1 Corinthians 10:31

Jesus said, "Anyone who chooses to do the will of God will find out whether my teaching comes from God or whether I speak on my own" (John 7:17). The essential prerequisite to knowing the will of God is a willingness to accept it before you know what it is. Suppose God's plan for your life is on the other side of a closed door and you ask, "What is it?" Why do you want to know? So you can decide whether or not you want to go through the door? If God is God, doesn't He have the right to decide what is on the other side?

17

If we don't give Him that right, we have usurped the throne of God and He is no longer the Lord of our lives. George Mueller wrote, "I seek at the beginning to get my heart into such a state that it has no will of its own in regard to a given matter. Nine-tenths of the difficulties are overcome when our hearts are ready to do the Lord's will, whatever it may be. When one is truly ready in this state, it is usually but a little way to the knowledge of what His will is."[1]

It is helpful to ask ourselves two questions when trying to discern God's will. First, will God be glorified if we do it? We glorify God when we bear fruit (see John 15:8), which includes the fruit of the Spirit and the fruit of reproduction. If what we are doing cannot be done without violating the fruit of the Spirit, it is best that we don't do it. This is the greatest test of our faith in public. In the face of temptation or hostile opposition, can we continue living by the Spirit, or will we defer to the flesh?

We are in the will of God if we maintain our position in Christ and let the fruit of the Spirit be evident in our lives. As long as we are within the moral boundaries of God, "all things are lawful," though "not all things are profitable" (1 Corinthians 10:23 NASB). In exercising our own freedom, we do not have the right to violate another person's conscience. We must restrict our freedom for the sake of the weaker Christian and always consider the good of others.

A second question relates to our witness. Can we do whatever is in question and be a positive witness for the Lord Jesus Christ? Paul says, "Though I am free and belong to no one, I have made myself a slave to everyone, to win as many as possible. To the Jews I became like a Jew, to win the Jews. . . . I have become all things to all people so that by all possible means I might save some. I do all this for the sake of the gospel, that I may share in its blessings (1 Corinthians 9:19–20, 22–23).

If we are compromising our witness, we cannot be in the center of God's will. There are many morally neutral activities in which we can participate, but sometimes we don't have the maturity to do so without giving in to old flesh patterns. In such cases, it is best not to participate in them until we have reached enough maturity to stay in God's will and exhibit the fruit of the Spirit.

Why do many people hesitate to fully yield their lives to God?

_____

_____

_____

Why must there be a willingness on our part to accept God's plan for our lives before we know what it is?

_____

_____

_____

_____

What two questions are important to ask when deciding whether something is right or wrong for ourselves?

_____

_____

_____

_____

What "morally neutral" activities have you avoided, or should you avoid, so as to not compromise your witness?

_____

_____

_____

_____

How convinced are you that God's will for your life is good, acceptable, and perfect for you?

_____

_____

_____

He [Jesus] tells them, you will fully know that "my doctrine" comes from God the Father when you choose to follow His will rather than yours. . . . The fact that Jesus does not teach anything foreign to the law is clear proof that He does not labor for His own glory through His teaching, for if He did, He would speak of Himself.

Cyril of Alexandria (AD 376–444)

3

Divine Guidance

2 Kings 2:1–25

Key Point

Set your course by the light of God's Word and not by the light of every passing ship.

Key Verse

For this God is our God for ever and ever; he will be our guide even to the end.

Psalm 48:14

Wherever God told Elijah to go, he went. However, when he ran from Jezebel he was misguided, so God led him to his replacement. The passing of the mantle from Elijah to Elisha is one of the most fascinating accounts of divine guidance in all of the Bible. Elisha had followed Elijah because God was with him, but now God was his master and Elisha would follow Him. How should we follow God?

Should we let our *consciences* be our guide? Our conscience is a function of our mind, and it can be defiled (see Titus 1:15). The Holy Spirit is our guide. Legalistic teaching can produce a guilty conscience, and a

21

pagan conscience would sense no guilt. Salvation and growth in Christ renew our minds and therefore our consciences. A conscience is always true to itself, not necessarily to the Word of God. However, in the process of being transformed by the renewing of our minds, we shouldn't violate our conscience, nor that of others. Paul says, "I strive always to keep my conscience clear before God and man" (Acts 24:16).

Should we ask God for a *sign*? The idea of placing a "fleece" before the Lord comes from chapter 6 in the book of Judges. Gideon asked God for a sign to confirm what He had already revealed. Gideon wasn't demonstrating faith in God. How many times does God need to say something before we are sure He means it? How much confirmation do we need in order to do what we know is right?

Should we be guided by the *circumstances* of life? Circumstances govern a lot of people's lives, but they are the least trustworthy. Assuming it isn't God's will if the circumstances are unfavorable and assuming it is God's will if the circumstances are favorable may be taking the path of least resistance. We need greater resolve to stay faithful when difficulties arise.

Should we seek the *counsel of others*? "For lack of guidance a nation falls, but victory is won through many advisers" (Proverbs 11:14). It is always wise to seek godly counsel and gain the perspective of others; however, "blessed is the one who does not walk in step with the wicked" (Psalm 1:1).

Should we be led by our *gifts and abilities*? God will always lead us in a way that is consistent with how He has equipped us. He will never ask us to be someone we aren't, nor will He lead us to do something we aren't qualified to do. God has led many faithful people with simple gifts and abilities to do amazing things. Because you can't do many things doesn't mean that God isn't leading you to do little things that multiply throughout His kingdom.

Should we be led by our *desires*? If we follow our natural desires, we will be led astray. However, if we "take delight in the LORD . . . he will give [us] the desires of [our] heart" (Psalm 37:4). If you delight yourself in the Lord your desires will be His desires.

Does *duty* call? Our calling is not to see what lies dimly ahead but to do what clearly lies at hand. We don't need any special leading to do our Christian duty. Nor do we need a subjective confirmation for doing what is clearly taught in Scripture.

What are the pros and cons of letting your conscience be your guide?

_____

_____

_____

What are the pros and cons of seeking guidance through signs and "fleeces"?

_____

_____

_____

What are the pros and cons of letting circumstances guide you? Of seeking guidance through the counsel of others?

_____

_____

_____

What are the pros and cons of letting your gifts and abilities guide you?

_____

_____

_____

What are the pros and cons of following your desires?

_____

_____

_____

"To have a clear conscience," he [Paul] says, "toward God and toward people." This is the perfection of virtue, when we give no cause for grudge to people and strive to give no offense to God.

John Chrysostom (AD 347–407)

4

Making Wise Decisions

Proverbs 3:13–24

Key Point

The wise person knows the will of God, but the successful person does it.

Key Verses

Be very careful, then, how you live—not as unwise but as wise, making the most of every opportunity, because the days are evil. Therefore do not be foolish, but understand what the Lord's will is.

Ephesians 5:15–17

In Deuteronomy 32:28–29, Moses said that Israel was "a nation without sense, there is no discernment in them. If only they were wise and would understand this and discern what their end would be." Like all the great spiritual leaders in the Bible, Moses was intimate with God and acquiesced to His will in all things. The *wise* person knows the will of God; the *successful* person does it. If you are trying to discern God's will and make wise decisions, consider the following questions.

First, *have you prayed about it*? The first thing a Christian does about anything is pray and seek God's kingdom. Recall that the Lord's Prayer begins with a petition to establish God's kingdom and do His will.

Second, *is what you are considering consistent with the message of the Bible?* God has already revealed the majority of His will for your life in His Word. Even in the courts of our land, ignorance of the law is no excuse. So make it your habit to consult the Bible when making decisions.

Third, *does the decision or choice compromise your Christian witness?* If the choice you are considering requires you to compromise your witness or integrity, then the answer is no. It is never right to do something wrong, even if you think something good may come of it. The end does not justify the means.

Fourth, *will the Lord be glorified through the act?* Are you seeking the glory of man or the glory of God? Can you do it and glorify God in your body? Are you concerned about God's reputation or yours? Are you building His kingdom or yours?

Fifth, *are you choosing and acting responsibly?* What is your responsibility, and what would be the most responsible course of action to take? You cannot be in God's will and shirk your responsibility. Making a wise and informed decision is part of your responsibility, and God won't make it for you.

Sixth, *does a reasonable opportunity exist?* God expects you to think. His guidance may transcend human reasoning, but it never collides with it. God's guidance never bypasses your mind; He operates through it. "Brothers and sisters, stop thinking like children. In regard to evil be infants, but in your thinking be adults" (1 Corinthians 14:20).

Seventh, *does a realistic opportunity exist?* Closed doors are not meant to be broken down. If you have a hopeless scheme, let it go. If a realistic opportunity exists, and all the other factors are in agreement, then step out in faith. God opens windows of opportunity, but they may close if you don't take advantage of them.

Eighth, *are unbiased, spiritually sensitive associates in agreement?* Be careful not to consult only with those who are inclined to agree with you or those who are afraid to be honest with you. Give people permission to ask hard questions and the right to disagree with you without recrimination.

Ninth, *do you have a sanctified desire to do it?* The greatest joy in life is to serve God and be in His will. You should feel good about doing God's will and want nothing less. God's guidance comes with a longing in your heart to do what you have been called to do.

Finally, *do you have a peace about it*? You should sense an inner confirmation if you are in God's will and a troubled spirit if you aren't.

How did Moses demonstrate that he was both a wise and successful leader?

Why is it important to *pray* and *examine your life* when seeking wisdom?

Decisions may have unintended consequences. How can considering the outcome of your actions help you make wise choices?

How does God work through your mind? How should your mind be engaged in the before and aftermath of decision-making?

Who among your associates would you go to for wise and godly counsel?

Christ, the Son of Righteousness, has risen. Rise up from the sleep of the age. Walk cautiously and prudently. Cast off folly. Take hold of wisdom. In this way you will be able to avoid changing yourself constantly as you walk through the vicissitudes of the times. Rather, you will find a unity within yourself even amid the diversity of the times.

Jerome (AD 347–420)

5

God Guides a
Moving Ship

Acts 16:1–10

Key Point

God's guidance comes when we are actively doing His will.

Key Verse

I thank Christ Jesus our Lord, who has given me strength, that he considered me trustworthy, appointing me to his service.

1 Timothy 1:12

In Acts 15:36–41, Paul and Silas embarked on a journey to revisit the churches that Paul had helped establish on his first missionary trip. The churches were being strengthened and increasing in numbers (see Acts 16:5). Suddenly, the Holy Spirit kept them from preaching in Asia, and the Spirit of Jesus would not allow them to keep going the same direction (see verses 6–7). Then Paul received a vision to go to Macedonia (see verse 9). If God had wanted Paul to go to Macedonia in the first place, why didn't He just guide Paul on a more direct path? The reason is that God wanted Paul to start his second missionary trip by strengthening the churches in Asia.

This midcourse correction underscores an important concept of divine guidance: God can only guide a moving ship. A rudder doesn't work if the ship isn't moving, and a ship without power is helpless at sea. The helmsman can't do anything with a motionless ship, because the rudder only works if the ship is under way. Likewise, guidance comes when we are actively doing God's will, not our will. Life is a journey that takes us through many bends in a river. Like a good river pilot, God guides us around obstacles and away from troubled waters. If we are actively serving God, we will experience many midcourse corrections. We may not know in advance where God is leading us, but we will never get there if we are not actively under way.

We also need to bloom where we have been planted, or further guidance may not be forthcoming. Rattling doors to find an open one is not God's way. We should be content where we are and prove ourselves faithful in what God has already assigned us to do. He will open the doors of opportunity at the right time. If we aren't bearing fruit now, it is unlikely that we will be fruitful in another time and place.

Isaiah wrote, "The Lord will guide you always" (58:11). In the verses prior to this text, Isaiah wrote that the Israelites had been seeking God's leading by fasting (see verses 2–3). However, God revealed their fasting to be a farce that ended in strife (see verse 4). He then shares what a real spiritual fast should be for those who are intent on discerning His will: "Is not this the kind of fasting I have chosen: to loose the chains of injustice and untie the cords of the yoke, to set the oppressed free and break every yoke? Is it not to share your food with the hungry and to provide the poor wanderer with shelter—when you see the naked, to clothe them, and not to turn away from your own flesh and blood? Then your light will break forth like the dawn" (verses 6–8).

In other words, God was asking the people why they were fasting to know His will when they had clearly not been faithful to do what He had already commanded them to do. If they would minister to His people the way that He had instructed, then their next step would be clear. If you show yourself faithful in little things, God will enlarge your ministry.

In Acts 16:1–10, how did God orchestrate a midcourse direction change during Paul's second missionary journey?

_____

_____

_____

_____

What is wrong with patiently waiting for God to guide us?

_____

_____

_____

How does being faithful to follow God's instructions lead to a better understanding of His will?

_____

_____

_____

_____

Have you ever had a "midcourse" correction? Do you need one?

_____

_____

_____

_____

What opportunities are you exploiting right now—or are you waiting for your "ship to come in"?

_____

_____

_____

"When he had seen the vision, immediately we sought to go on to Macedonia, concluding that God had called us. . . ." And notice how it says, "a man of Macedonia was standing beseeching him and saying." Not "ordering" but "beseeching"; that is, on behalf of the very people needing caring. What does "concluding" mean? It means they made an inference. From the fact that Paul saw him and not someone else, that Paul was "forbidden by the Holy Spirit" and that they were at the borders—from all this they reached a conclusion.

John Chrysostom (AD 347–407)

Faith Appraisal (Part 1)

One of our sons, Mike, wanted to take private speech (he's such a talker anyway, I recommended "hush" instead). But it was inexpensive, and he was interested, so we let him. The climax of the year's labor was a two-hour long assortment of clowns, kings, rabbits, and forgotten lines known as the Speech Recital given to a devoted audience of eager parents and trapped friends.

Mike was a king. He looked rather regal too, if I do say so myself. At least until the queen, a head taller and twenty pounds heavier, stood beside him casting a pall on his regality. He had only three lines to say—nine months of speech, three short lines—and they came very late, in the last moment of the last act of the very last play. Any way you looked at it, he was not the star—at least to anyone except a couple about halfway back on the left side.

It was a long evening and it was miserably hot, but Mike waited. He was ready and said his lines, and he said them well. Not too soon, not too late, not too loud, not too soft, but just right—he said his lines.

I'm just a bit player too, not a star in any way, but God gave me a line or so in the pageant of life. When the curtain falls and the drama ends—and the stage is vacant at last—I don't ask for a critic's raves or fame in any amount. I only hope that God can say, "He said his lines, not too soon, not too late, not too loud, not too soft. He said his lines, and he said them well."[1]

—Bob Benson, *Laughter in the Walls*

Daily Readings

1. The Plumb Line	Amos 7:1–9
2. Success	Joshua 1:1–9
3. Significance	Ecclesiastes 3:1–11
4. Fulfillment	Habakkuk 3:16–19
5. Satisfaction	Ecclesiastes 5:8–12

1

The Plumb Line

Amos 7:1–9

Key Point

People don't always live according to what they profess, but they do live according to what they actually believe.

Key Verse

For in the gospel the righteousness of God is revealed—a righteousness that is by faith from first to last, just as it is written: "The righteous will live by faith."

Romans 1:17

A "plumb line" is a tool that consists of a small weight attached to a string or a rope. Carpenters use plumb lines to ensure that the walls of a structure are built straight. The Lord showed Amos that the nation of Israel was no longer true to His plumb line (see Amos 7:7–8). God's people were supposed to be built by His standards. However, when tested they were found to be completely out of plumb.

God desires that we live a successful, significant, fulfilling, and satisfied life. Whether we do (or not) is totally dependent on what we believe. The readings in this session and the next will help you determine how true your plumb line is. Start by assessing your own walk of faith with the following appraisal. Circle the number that best represents you, and then complete the statements.

Question/Statement	Low				High
1. How successful am I? I would be more successful if . . .	1	2	3	4	5
2. How significant am I? I would be more significant if . . .	1	2	3	4	5
3. How fulfilled am I? I would be more fulfilled if . . .	1	2	3	4	5
4. How satisfied am I? I would be more satisfied if . . .	1	2	3	4	5
5. How encouraged am I? I would be more encouraged if . . .	1	2	3	4	5
6. How happy am I? I would be happier if . . .	1	2	3	4	5
7. How much fun am I having? I would have more fun if . . .	1	2	3	4	5
8. How secure am I? I would be more secure if . . .	1	2	3	4	5

9. How peaceful am I?   1   2   3   4   5

    I would be more peaceful if . . .

However you completed the above sentences reflects what you presently believe, and you are right now living according to what you have chosen to believe. Are your beliefs consistent with Scripture?

It is hard to image that a loving heavenly Father has called us to be failing, insignificant, unfulfilled, and dissatisfied children of God. It is possible to score a five on all nine issues above—the deciding factor is what you believe. How you are doing is dependent on your relationship with God and your walk by faith. The fact that nobody and nothing can keep you from being the person God created you to be is what makes that possible.

How stable is any building program if the plumb line is wrong? How does that relate to faith?

Why do we need to occasionally take a self-inventory?

What other "plumb lines" besides the Bible do people have that influence what they believe?

Do you truly believe that God wants you to live a successful, significant, fulfilled, and satisfied life? Why or why not?

How important is it to you that your profession of faith matches what you really believe? Why?

Before all things, keep that truth which is committed to your trust, the Holy Word of faith by which you have been taught and instructed. And let no weeds of heresy grow up among you, but preserve the heavenly seed pure and sincere, that it may yield a great harvest to the Master, when He comes to demand an account of our lives.

John of Damascus (AD 675–749)

2

Success

Joshua 1:1–9

Key Point

Success is knowing God, accepting His goal for our lives, and, by His grace, becoming the person He created us to be.

Key Verse

Dear friend, I pray that you may enjoy good health and that all may go well with you, even as your soul is getting along well.

3 John 1:2

Success is related to goals, but how are we setting realistic and godly personal goals for our lives? What may be a realistic goal for one person could be impossible for another. God has not given each person the same endowment of gifts, talents, and intelligence. In addition, our identity and sense of worth are not determined by those qualities. Our sense of worth is based on our identity in Christ and our growth in character—both of which are equally accessible to every child of God. Success is accepting God's goal for our lives and, by His grace, becoming what He created us to be.

We can be successful in the eyes of the world but be a complete failure in the eyes of God, and vice versa. Many have climbed the ladder of success only to realize that it was leaning against the wrong wall. The first principle of success is to know God and His Word and live accordingly. Paul said, "I consider everything a loss because of the surpassing worth of knowing Christ Jesus my Lord" (Philippians 3:8). God instructed Joshua, "Be strong and very courageous. Be careful to obey all the law my servant Moses gave you; do not turn from it to the right or to the left, that you may be successful wherever you go. Keep this Book of the Law always on your lips; meditate on it day and night, so that you may be careful to do everything written in it. Then you will be prosperous and successful" (Joshua 1:7–8).

The Israelites' success did not depend on the cooperation of the Philistines or favorable circumstances. They stepped into the water by faith and crossed the Jordan River (see Joshua 3). They were successful in defeating the city of Jericho by faith (see Joshua 6). However, the Israelites were defeated at Ai because a man named Achan violated God's command (see Joshua 7:10–12). This first principle of success is a faith stretcher. Do you believe that you could run for public office and win or be a successful businessperson without violating the Word of God? Success may mean that you are an honest person who drives a less expensive car and lives in a modest home.

The second principle of success is to become the people God created us to be. We may not have enough time to accomplish what we set out to do, but we have precisely enough time to do God's will. We may not be able to reach some "prestigious" social position, but what position is higher than being seated with Christ in the heavenlies? We can try to make a name for ourselves in this world, but would that surpass being called a child of God? Scripture provides no instruction for determining our career, but it gives a lot of instruction about what kind of career person we should be.

Being good stewards of our time, talent, and treasure is the third principle of success. The Lord wants us to prosper, but what is our definition of prosperity? What material possession or social status would you exchange for love, joy, peace, patience, kindness, goodness, faithfulness, gentleness, and self-control? No earthly possession or position can give us what we inwardly desire, which is equally available to all God's children if we just abide in Christ.

In Joshua 3, why do you think God told those carrying the ark to step into the water first, and then He would roll back the water?

_____

_____

_____

Why is successfully reaching temporal goals so fleeting?

_____

_____

_____

How is God's definition of success different from the world's definition?

_____

_____

_____

How does your answer to "I would be successful if . . ." compare to God's definition of success?

_____

_____

_____

_____

What part of the Christian faith have you been willing to compromise in order to reach your own goals?

_____

_____

_____

If we think only of ourselves, we may act for our own benefit and bother only with our own affairs, our hope, our own deliverance. But this is not enough. We are truly acting for ourselves if we also have a concern for others and strive to be of benefit to them. For since we are all one body, we look out for ourselves when we look out for others.

Gaius Marius Victorinus (c. fourth century AD)

3

Significance

Ecclesiastes 3:1–11

Key Point

What is forgotten in time is of little significance, but what is remembered for eternity is highly significant.

Key Verse

If what has been built survives, the builder will receive a reward.

1 Corinthians 3:14

Significance is related to time and eternity. What is forgotten in time is of little significance, but what is remembered for eternity is of great significance. God has set eternity in our hearts and appointed a time for everything (see Ecclesiastes 3:1, 11). If we want to increase our significance, then we should focus our energies on those activities that have lasting value. Paul writes, "For physical training is of some value, but godliness has value for all things, holding promise for both the present life and the life to come" (1 Timothy 4:8).

There are two misplaced priorities concerning the concept of significance. The first is the significance the world attaches to things that don't stand the test of time and are irrelevant in eternity, such as sporting events, movies, and rock concerts. They may impact the world for a season of time, but they are soon lost to history. What countries participated in the World Cup of soccer fifteen years ago? Who won the World Series in baseball twenty years ago? Who was the most valuable player in that game? Who cares?

The world tries to maintain the significance of athletic events by keeping records, but the general population soon forgets all about them. It was a significant achievement for humankind when Neil Armstrong landed on the moon, but now flights into space barely make the headlines. Many young people don't even know who Neil Armstrong is!

The second misplaced priority is the sense of insignificance that Christians feel concerning their service for God. The world makes such a big deal about "significant" events that quickly fade from memory, while the daily events of one Christian or local church go unnoticed. However, what happens in heaven when one sinner repents? All the angels in heaven rejoice. Jesus said, "I tell you that in the same way there will be more rejoicing in heaven over one sinner who repents than over ninety-nine righteous persons who do not need to repent" (Luke 15:7). That person's name is now written in the Lamb's Book of Life, and he or she will live in the presence of God forever.

Someone teaching a group of little children in church may feel insignificant compared to the stars of Hollywood or the celebrities in music and sports. Yet what could be more significant than teaching a young child the truth? What children choose to believe now will affect them for all eternity.

There is no need to search for significance, because there are no insignificant children of God. There are no insignificant Christian ministries—no matter how obscure—provided that they are doing God's will. We are in the significant business of laying up for ourselves "treasures in heaven, where moths and vermin do not destroy, and where thieves do not break in and steal" (Matthew 6:20). We will live significant lives if we build on the foundation that Christ has laid, but everything we build for ourselves in our own strength will be torn down.

As the British missionary Charles T. Studd once said, "Only one life, 'twill soon be past, only what is done for Christ will last. And when I am dying, how happy I'll be, if the lamp of my life has been burned out for Thee."[1] The ability to postpone rewards is a sign of maturity and success.

What does it mean that God has "set eternity in the human heart"?

_____

_____

_____

_____

Why is significance related to "what lasts"?

_____

_____

_____

_____

What are the two misplaced priorities concerning significance?

_____

_____

_____

What types of activities make you feel the most significant?

_____

_____

_____

_____

How should you prioritize your activities (even in the temporal world, such as earning a degree as opposed to attending an entertainment venue) so that your energies are focused more toward events and accomplishments that last for years and for eternity?

With a single heart, therefore, and exclusively for the sake of the kingdom of heaven, we ought to do good to all. And in this well-doing we ought not to think about temporal rewards, either exclusively or conjointly with the kingdom of God. For it is with reference to all these temporal things that the Lord used the word "tomorrow" when He said, "Do not think about tomorrow." For that word is not used except in the realm of time, where the future succeeds the past. Therefore, when we perform any good deed, let us think about eternal things and pay no heed to the temporal. Then our deed will be not only good but perfect.

Augustine of Hippo (AD 354–430)

4

Fulfillment

Habakkuk 3:16–19

Key Point

Fulfillment is discovering your own uniqueness in Christ and using your gifts and talents to edify others and glorify the Lord.

Key Verse

He fulfills the desires of those who fear him; he hears their cry and saves them.

Psalm 145:19

Fulfillment is related to your calling in life. God has a place of ministry for you, and it is important to your sense of fulfillment to realize what that is. Fulfillment is discovering your own uniqueness in Christ and using your gifts and talents to edify others and glorify the Lord. Start by considering the roles you occupy in which you cannot be replaced. For instance, there are more than seven billion people in this world, but you are the only person who can be someone's sister, brother, father, mother, co-worker, neighbor, or special friend.

One mother was puzzled by young ladies who entered the workforce to find their fulfillment in the world. She thought, *What could be more fulfilling, challenging, or rewarding than to raise godly children in this world?* A businessman wondered about his co-workers who stepped on each other's backs and neglected their families in order to get ahead so that they could be "fulfilled" in their work. He thought, *What can be more fulfilling than to be a good witness at work, where I serve the Lord and make provision for my family?*

We all occupy a unique role as ambassadors for Christ where we live, work, and play. These are our mission fields, and we are the workers whom God has appointed for the harvest. Our greatest fulfillment comes from accepting and occupying God's unique place for us to the best of our ability. We can always pray for the people in our world and look for opportunities to share the love of Christ with them. We may be their only link to the Church and to the gospel of the Lord Jesus Christ.

As we search for our role in life and in the Church, we must be on the lookout for any potential cause for lack of fulfillment. We must not fall into the trap of the young student who once quizzed his teacher, "What is my spiritual gift—prophecy or exhortation?" The teacher replied, "I don't think it is either one. If anyone has the gift of service, you certainly do. I have seen you move instinctively to meet the needs of others." The disappointed student replied, "I knew it." We will never be fulfilled trying to become somebody we aren't, seeking gifts that others have, or aspiring to a ministry we are not qualified to do. The only way to be fulfilled in life is to discover our own potential and uniqueness in Christ and become that to the glory of God.

Jesus fulfilled His calling even though there was so much more that others wanted Him to do. In His last breath, He was able to say, "It is finished" (John 19:30). Paul also fulfilled his calling. "I have fought the good fight, I have finished the race, I have kept the faith" (2 Timothy 4:7). He said to Timothy, "But you, be sober in all things, endure hardship, do the work of an evangelist, fulfill your ministry" (2 Timothy 4:5 NASB). Habakkuk felt fulfilled as he concluded his work: "I will be joyful in God my Savior. The Sovereign LORD is my strength; he makes my feet like the feet of a deer, he enables me to tread on the heights" (Habakkuk 3:18–19). In the midst of dire circumstances, that is one of the strongest affirmations of faith in all of the Bible.

How is fulfillment related to a person's unique calling in life?

As believers in Christ, how can we find fulfillment in any situation where God has placed us?

What is the harm in trying to be someone we aren't or in seeking something God never intended us to have?

Which of your daily activities do you find to be most fulfilling? Why?

How can life be more fulfilling for you?

For in a contest there is much labor needed. After the contest victory falls to some, but to others disgrace. Is the palm ever given or the crown granted before the course is finished? Paul writes well when he says, "I have fought the good fight, I have finished the course, I have kept the faith; henceforth there is laid up for me a crown of righteousness, which the Lord, the righteous judge, shall give me at that day; and not to me only, but to all who love His appearing."

Ambrose (AD 340–397)

5

Satisfaction

Ecclesiastes 5:8–12

Key Point

Quality relationships and righteous living breed satisfaction.

Key Verse

Blessed are those who hunger and thirst for righteousness, for they shall be satisfied.

Matthew 5:6 NASB

Solomon wrote, "Whoever loves money never has enough; whoever loves wealth is never satisfied with their income. This too is meaningless" (Ecclesiastes 5:10). Money is power to the worldly, and it enables them to purchase what they want. Very few people today could compare to Solomon's wealth and power, yet even he wasn't satisfied—and he had the wisdom to understand that. Jesus said, "Blessed are those who hunger and thirst for righteousness, for they shall be satisfied" (Matthew 5:6 NASB). If you believed that, what would you be doing?

What causes individuals to be dissatisfied is seldom related to what enables them to be satisfied. When people complain about the potholes in the roads, the hard chairs at church, or the temperature of the auditorium, are they satisfied when their complaints are heard and the problems fixed? Maybe for a short time, but they will soon find something else to complain about because they are dissatisfied with life. This is why it is so unproductive for church leaders to run around putting out fires. As soon as one is out, another one will start. These leaders are investing their time in that which causes dissatisfaction and not on what causes people to be satisfied. What satisfies people are meaningful ministries that bear fruit and quality relationships with God and others. Seldom will you see a Christian bearing fruit who isn't satisfied.

Quality is the key to satisfaction. Satisfaction comes from living righteously and seeking to raise the level of quality in relationships, service, and products. To raise the level of satisfaction, you have to focus on raising the quality. Have you ever been satisfied with an inferior product you made? Have you ever been satisfied with a poor performance or service? You will be a lot more satisfied if you do a few things well than a lot of things in a mediocre way. The same holds true for relationships. You don't need a lot of superficial friends. "One who has unreliable friends soon comes to ruin, but there is a friend who sticks closer than a brother" (Proverbs 18:24).

We all need a few close friends who value a quality relationship. What about your most important earthly relationship—your marriage relationship? If you are not satisfied in your marriage, you will not solve it with gifts or promises. You will only solve it by being reconciled to God and each other in a righteous way. That is why superficial reconciliation leaves everybody dissatisfied. Materialists strive for quality possessions and invest a lot in maintaining them, but that doesn't equate to quality of life. If they put the same amount of energy and time into quality relationships, they would be a lot more satisfied.

Quality, not quantity, is what Jesus modeled. He occasionally taught the multitudes (see Mark 6:34), and He did equip seventy-two workers (see Luke 10:1–17), but He invested most of His time with His twelve disciples. Out of those twelve, He selected only three to be with Him on the Mount of Transfiguration (see Mark 9:2) and the Garden of Gethsemane (see Mark 14:32–33). Finally, there was only one who stayed with Jesus at the foot of the cross—John—and to this disciple, Jesus entrusted the care of His mother (see John 19:26–27).

Why are so many people, who have so many things, so dissatisfied?

_____

_____

_____

Why is the focus on resolving people's dissatisfactions a futile pursuit?

_____

_____

_____

Why is quality and not quantity the key to satisfaction?

_____

_____

_____

How did your answer to "I would be more satisfied if . . ." compare to this lesson?

_____

_____

_____

How can you raise your level of satisfaction?

_____

_____

_____

Abundance does not yield either knowledge or virtue. How so? Because just as penury [oppressive lack of resources] occasions much wrongdoing, so does plenty. Many who have become affluent have become derelict. They do not know how to bear good fortune. But not so with Paul, for what he received he spent on others. He emptied himself for others.

John Chrysostom (AD 347–407)

Faith Appraisal (Part 2)

I think we have lost the old knowledge that happiness is overrated—that, in a way, life is overrated. We have lost, somehow, a sense of mystery—about us, our purpose, our meaning, our role. Our ancestors believed in two worlds and understood this to be the solitary, poor, nasty, brutish, and short one. We are the first generations of man that actually expected to find happiness here on earth, and our search for it has caused such unhappiness. The reason? If you do not believe in another, higher world—if you believe only in the flat material world around you, if you believe that this is your only chance at happiness—if that is what you believe, then you are not disappointed when the world does not give you a good measure of its riches, you are despairing.[1]

—Peggy Noonan, speechwriter for
President Ronald Reagan and George W. Bush

Daily Readings

1. Encouragement	Nehemiah 4:1–23
2. Happiness	Ecclesiastes 11:7–10
3. Fun	2 Samuel 6:1–23
4. Security	Psalm 23:1–6
5. Peace	Isaiah 32:9–20

1

Encouragement

Nehemiah 4:1–23

Key Point

Encouragement gives us and others the courage to run the race with endurance.

Key Verse

Therefore encourage one another and build each other up, just as in fact you are doing.

1 Thessalonians 5:11

The world is filled with "blessing snatchers." These are the individuals who can find something bad in everything. They feel called to play the role of the devil's advocate, even though the devil doesn't need any help. They are quick to object and always have a reason why something can't be done. Dripping with negativity, they put a damper on life. Many of these pessimistic people who see only the dark side of life probably don't realize how discouraging they are to others. Sanballat and Tobiah in Nehemiah 4 represent the worst of these types, as they oppose the work of God and ridicule those who are trying to do God's will. "What they are building—even a fox climbing up on it would break down their wall of stones!" (verse 3).

Nehemiah was an encourager. Encouragers motivate others to courageously continue on. When Nehemiah heard the insults of Sanballat and Tobiah, he prayed (see verse 4), and the people continued working with all their hearts. This only caused the enemy to unite against them, but Nehemiah prayed again and then stationed guards. The enemy continued to chip away by spreading lies.

Propaganda is an effective weapon in war. An army can be defeated without weapons if they become discouraged and believe the lies of the enemy. Listen to the discouraging tone of the rumor mill: "The strength of the laborers is giving out, and there is so much rubble that we cannot rebuild the wall. Also our enemies said, 'Before they know it or see us, we will be right there among them and will kill them and put an end to the work'" (verses 10–11). Such is the work of terrorists in this world.

Nehemiah countered again by stationing half the people for defensive purposes. Then he gave a speech to all the people and said, "Don't be afraid of them. Remember the Lord, who is great and awesome, and fight for your families, your sons and your daughters, your wives and your homes" (verse 14). The people's fear was abated when they remembered the Lord, and they returned to their task of rebuilding the wall. God had frustrated the plans of the enemy (see verse 15). When the walls were completed and the enemy heard about it, "all the surrounding nations were afraid and lost their self-confidence, because they realized that this work had been done with the help of our God" (Nehemiah 6:16).

We may not have leaders like Nehemiah to encourage us, but we can always encourage ourselves in the Lord as David did when he was "greatly distressed . . . but David found strength in the LORD his God" (1 Samuel 30:6). When we feel discouraged, we should remember that God is great and awesome. He will meet all our needs, and we can do everything through Christ who strengthens us (see Philippians 4:13, 19). Therefore, "let us consider how we may spur one another on toward love and good deeds, not giving up meeting together, as some are in the habit of doing, but encouraging one another—and all the more as you see the Day approaching" (Hebrews 10:24–25). When you encourage someone, you give that person the courage to run the race with endurance.

What effect did the words of Sanballat and Tobiah have on the people of Israel?

How did Nehemiah seek to counter this attack from the enemy? What can we learn from that?

What are some of the avenues for discouragement?

What or who has caused discouragement in your life?

How can you go from being a "blessing snatcher" to being an encourager?

"But encourage one another daily, as long as it is called Today" *[Hebrews 3:13]. He said "today" that they might never be without hope. "Exhort one another daily," he says. That is, even if persons have sinned, as long as it is "today," they have hope; let them not then despair so long as they live. Above all things indeed, he says, "Let there not be an evil, unbelieving heart." But even if there should be, let no one despair, but let that one recover; for as long as we are in this world "today" is in season.*

John Chrysostom (AD 347–407)

2

Happiness

Ecclesiastes 11:7–10

Key Point

Happy are those who want what they have.

Key Verse

Go and enjoy choice food and sweet drinks, and send some to those who have nothing prepared. This day is holy to our Lord. Do not grieve, for the joy of the LORD is your strength.

Nehemiah 8:10

Solomon encourages us to enjoy life while we are living (especially in our youth), because the darkness of death is coming. Earlier, Solomon tells us that enjoying life includes eating and drinking (see Ecclesiastes 2:24; 3:13; 8:15; 9:7), wearing nice clothes and pleasant lotions (see 9:8), enjoying marital bliss (see 9:9), and finding satisfaction in our work (see 2:24; 3:22; 5:18). We should do what our hearts desire, but first we must delight ourselves in the Lord so that our desires are in line with the joy of the Lord.

Wanting what we have is the key to happiness. Think about it. All commercialization is based on the premise that we would be happy if we only had what they are selling. Never has there been a time in human history when so many people have had so many material possessions and entertainment options and yet so many are unhappy. God's concept of happiness is summed up in the simple little proverb, "Happy are those who want what they have!" Then we will be happy all our lives. The problem is that we focus on what we don't have instead of on what we do have. Sad are those who want their own way and are driven by the belief they will be happy if they get it. Those who bear the brunt of their efforts will wonder, *Are you happy now?*

Consider what we deserve. If God gave us what we deserved, we would all suffer eternal damnation in hell. Now consider what we have. We have eternal life in Christ Jesus. We have the forgiveness of sins. We have the internal presence of the Holy Spirit, who leads us and enables us to live liberated lives in Christ. We have new life and a rich inheritance in Him. We have a God who will meet all our needs and will never leave us or forsake us. The Church used to sing, "Count your blessings; name them one by one. Count your many blessings, see what God has done."

Happiness can be so fleeting, because it is dependent on the circumstances of life. But we can always be joyful in our spirit when we know that the joy of the Lord is our strength (see Nehemiah 8:10). Personal happiness is the wrong goal. The goal is to know God, become the person He has created us to be, and let Him have His way. That leads only to godliness and contentment. "But godliness with contentment is great gain. For we brought nothing into the world, and we can take nothing out of it. But if we have food and clothing, we will be content with that" (1 Timothy 6:6–8).

God is joyful, and joy is a fruit of the Spirit. The joy that comes from knowing God is the result of your being at one with Him. Only in Christ can you say, "Rejoice always, pray continually, give thanks in all circumstances; for this is God's will for you in Christ Jesus" (1 Thessalonians 5:16–18). "Though you have not seen him, you love him; and even though you do not see him now, you believe in him and are filled with an inexpressible and glorious joy, for you are receiving the goal of your faith, the salvation of your souls" (1 Peter 1:8–9).

Are people happy when they get all the products and services they want?
Why or why not? How long will they be happy?

Why aren't people who always get their own way always happy? How happy
are those who have to live with such people?

Is happiness a product of the environment? Can we make others happy?
How?

Do you consider yourself a truly happy person? Why or why not?

How can you make the joy of the Lord your strength?

When the mind is freed from lust, established in tranquility and does not waver in its intention toward the one supreme good, the monk [saint] will fulfill the precept of St. Paul. "Pray without ceasing," and, "In every place lifting up holy hands without wrath and controversy." By purity of heart the mind is drawn away from earthly feelings and is re-formed in the likeness of an angelic spirit. Then, whatever thought the mind receives, whatever it considers, whatever it does, will be a prayer of true purity and sincerity.

John Cassian (AD 360–435)

3

Fun

2 Samuel 6:1–23

Key Point

Fun is uninhibited spontaneity.

Key Verse

The righteous shout for joy and are glad.

Proverbs 29:6

Fun is uninhibited spontaneity. Life is fun when we feel free and allow ourselves to be spontaneous. Worldly people plan their calendar around "fun" events. Have you ever planned a major "fun" event and asked yourself halfway through, *Are we having fun yet?* Many have made fun their chief ambition in life. They throw off their inhibitions by going to places where nobody cares how they act. Some believe they need to drink or take drugs to get rid of their inhibitions or escape from the dismal realities of their natural life. They think that Christians can't have any fun, because their "rules" keep them from being spontaneous and their "religion" makes them feel inhibited. That is a false understanding of a Christian's relationship with God, as David demonstrated.

David was bringing the ark of the covenant back to Jerusalem, and his joy was so great that he was "leaping and dancing before the LORD" (2 Samuel 6:16). This uninhibited spontaneity caused Michal, David's first wife and the daughter of Saul, to despise him in her heart. She said to David, "How the king of Israel has distinguished himself today" (verse 20). David had not been acting properly according to protocol, because he didn't have the typical inhibitions that plague those who are more concerned about what others think than what God thinks. However, God judged Michal, not David (see verse 23).

As David danced before the Lord, it didn't bother him that he was undignified in Michal's eyes. He didn't even care if he was humiliated in his own eyes (see verse 22). He was having fun in the presence of the Lord. Likewise, our lives will be a lot more fun if we rid ourselves of unscriptural inhibitors. Chief among the inhibitors of Christian fun is our carnal tendency to keep up appearances. We don't want to look out of place or be thought less of by others, so we stifle our inhibitions and spontaneity with a form of false decorum. That is people pleasing, and Paul said that anybody who lives to please people is not a bondservant of Christ (see Galatians 1:10). As Christians, we don't play for the grandstand. We play for the coach.

Too many Christians are sound in the faith but sour in the face. They claim to have the joy of the Lord, but you would never guess it by their countenance. Having fun in the presence of God is living with enthusiasm. "Enthusiasm" is derived from the words *en* (in) and *theos* (God), and literally means to be "in God." So it is not inconsistent for Christians to have fun and be enthusiastic about life. We are not chained to contemporary cultural taboos; we are liberated children of God. There is no need for us to keep up with the Joneses, because they probably don't have a clue where they are going. They may be without God and headed down the wrong path, but we're not. The world may be getting worse, but we're not.

So, how are we supposed to act? Christianity is not an *act*. It is a real *experience*. A liberated life in Christ. We restrict our freedom for our weaker brothers and sisters, but we don't act like the weaker brothers and sisters who can't be themselves. Frankly, it is fun being saved!

What would be more fun—standing in line at Disneyland or having a pillow fight with your children or grandchildren? Why is that? Which one costs the most? Which one feels better at the end of the day?

_____

_____

_____

_____

What is fun about being a liberated child of the God who judged Michal and not David when he danced before Him?

_____

_____

_____

What are some of the unscriptural inhibitors that plague the church?

_____

_____

_____

Do you feel free to spontaneously be yourself in Christian circles? Why or why not?

_____

_____

_____

_____

How can you increase your enthusiasm?

_____

_____

_____

So what should we pray for? "Ask in my name." And He did not say what for, but in His words we can understand what we ought to ask for. "Ask, and you will receive, that your joy may be full." . . . Ask for what can finally satisfy you. Because sometimes you ask for nothing. "Whoever drinks of this water will be thirsty again." You lower the bucket of greed into the well, you pull up something to drink, and you will again be thirsty. "Ask, so that your joy may be full"; that is, so you may be permanently satisfied.

Augustine of Hippo (AD 354–430)

4

Security
Psalm 23:1–6

Key Point

Security is related more to eternal truth than temporal things that we have no right or ability to control.

Key Verses

When you believed, you were marked in him with a seal, the promised Holy Spirit, who is a deposit guaranteeing our inheritance until the redemption of those who are God's possession—to the praise of his glory.

Ephesians 1:13–14

God is shaking the foundations of this world. Nations are rising and falling, uniting and dividing—and at a pace never observed before. Every day we hear of another country or region suffering political chaos, and many more that are suffering from economic insecurity. During the twentieth century alone, the population in the world has grown from 1.6 billion to 7 billion people.[1] Of all the people who have ever lived on earth, one half are alive today.

However, while the population is exploding, our natural resources are decreasing. This trend cannot continue without serious ramifications for our overcrowded planet. Consequently, there is a growing sense of insecurity all over the world. People are insecure because they are depending on temporal things over which they have no right or ability to control. Yet in the midst of ensuing conflicts, we have a Shepherd who will guide us even through the valley of the shadow of death (see Psalm 23:4).

Our security is rooted in eternity and not to the temporal and transitory things of this world. We are secure in Christ, and our security is found in our eternal relationship with Him. No one can snatch us out of our heavenly Father's hand (see John 10:35–39), and nothing can separate us from the love of God (see Romans 8:35–39). We were marked in Christ with a seal, the promised Holy Spirit, who is a deposit guaranteeing our inheritance (see Ephesians 1:13–14). It is inevitable that we will have conflicts in this world, but in the midst of them we can have a sense of security. Consider the following approaches to conflict:

Those who have a high regard for relationships and want to accomplish something seek to *resolve* conflicts. Others *yield* to the opposition for the sake of relationships if their need to achieve isn't that great. Those who have a high need to achieve but a low regard for relationships strive to *win* the battle. Those who have no regard for relationships and no desire to achieve simply *withdraw* when conflicts arise. Choosing to compromise is okay unless it means compromising what we believe.

Secure people are those who seek to *resolve* conflicts or yield for the sake of relationships. This is because security is found in relationships, not in achievements. Growing up, you probably felt secure in your family if relationships were valued over achievements. Secure individuals don't always have to be right and win every time there is a conflict, nor do they walk away from meaningful relationships. They have found their security in their eternal relationship with God and in their relationships with others. They are fulfilling the Great Commandment, which is to love God with all your heart and love your neighbor as yourself.

What situations and events in our world today make people feel insecure?

_____

_____

_____

What is the value of having an eternal perspective on life?

_____

_____

_____

How should Christians respond to external and temporal conflict?

_____

_____

_____

Considering the diagram above, how did your mother respond to conflict? How did your father respond to conflict? Which one are you most like?

_____

_____

_____

_____

What was valued the most in your upbringing: achievement or relationship? How has that impacted you?

Paul shows that while we are still in the world and not yet departed from this life we are already living amid God's promises. For through hope we are already in heaven. . . . As the anchor, dropped from the vessel, does not allow it to be carried about even if ten thousand winds agitate it but, being dependent upon, makes it steady, so also does hope.

John Chrysostom (AD 347–407)

5

Peace

Isaiah 32:9–20

Key Point

Peace is related to the internal order of our lives and not to the external disorder of the world.

Key Verse

Those who walk uprightly enter into peace.

Isaiah 57:2

Everybody wants peace in this world, but that might not always be possible. Peaceful coexistence is a desire that we all share, but it is not our primary goal. What frustrated parent doesn't want peace in the home? The only way you can guarantee that is to control every other member in the household, which you have no right or ability to do. Paul said, "If it is possible, as far as it depends on you, live at peace with everyone" (Romans 12:18). It isn't always possible, however, because achieving peace doesn't just depend on you.

Jesus said that we should "seek first his kingdom and his righteousness, and all these things will be given to you as well" (Matthew 6:33). Isaiah said, "The fruit of that righteousness will be peace" (32:17). That kind of peace is related to our internal order, not to the external order of this world. Jesus said, "I have told you these things, so that in me you may have peace. In this world you will have trouble. But take heart! I have overcome the world" (John 16:33).

Peace *on* earth is what we want, but peace *with* God is something we already have. "Therefore, since we have been justified through faith, we have peace with God through our Lord Jesus Christ" (Romans 5:1). The peace *of* God that guards our hearts and our minds in Christ Jesus is something we need to appropriate on a daily basis (see Philippians 4:7). The only One who can give us that peace is the Prince of Peace. Jesus said, "Peace I leave with you; my peace I give you. I do not give to you as the world gives. Do not let your hearts be troubled and do not be afraid" (John 14:27). The peace of Christ that rules in our hearts stands in stark contrast to the false prophets of this world. "They dress the wound of my people as though it were not serious. 'Peace, peace,' they say, when there is no peace. Are they ashamed of their detestable conduct? No, they have no shame at all; they do not even know how to blush" (Jeremiah 6:14–15).

We should pray for the peace of Jerusalem and for all the troubled spots in the world. We should seek to unite this world in peaceful reconciliation, because Jesus said, "Blessed are the peacemakers, for they will be called children of God" (Matthew 5:9). Peace can be humanly negotiated so that we can coexist without destroying ourselves, but that kind of peace only heals superficial wounds. The tension will always be there unless we resolve the inner conflicts. To accomplish inner peace, we have to work toward righteousness, and "its effect will be quietness and confidence forever" (Isaiah 32:17). We can have an inner peace in the midst of an external storm.

Peace comes when you quiet your heart before the Lord. In the midst of confusion, acknowledge God's presence in your life—a discipline the Quakers used to refer to as "centering down"—and then join in this prayer by John Greenleaf Whittier, one of America's most famous Quakers: "Drop Thy still dews of quietness, till all our strivings cease; take from our souls the strain and stress, and let our ordered lives confess, the beauty of Thy peace."[1]

Why is peaceful coexistence in this world not always possible to attain?

_____

_____

_____

How does the peace God offers differ from the peace that the false prophets of this world offer?

_____

_____

_____

How can we have the peace of God in the midst of external chaos?

_____

_____

_____

How could you "center down" and find peace on a daily basis?

_____

_____

_____

How could you be a peacemaker at home, church, and work?

_____

_____

_____

The person of peace ought to seek peace and follow it. The one who knows and loves the bond of charity ought to refrain his tongue from the evil of dissension. Among His divine commands and salutary teachings, the Lord, when He was very near to His passion, added this one, saying, "Peace I leave with you, my peace I give unto you." He gave this to us as an inheritance. He promised all the gifts and rewards of which He spoke through the preservation of peace. If we are fellow heirs with Christ, let us abide in the peace of Christ. If we are children of God, we ought to be peacemakers.

Cyprian (AD 200–258)

Spiritual Leadership

Once upon a time, there were three pastors. One was a Methodist pastor who was an Arminian, and he believed that a person could lose his or her salvation. Another was a Presbyterian pastor who was a Calvinist, and he believed that true saints are elected and therefore cannot lose their salvation. The third was a charismatic pastor, and he just believed!

One tragic day they all died, and to their surprise they ended up in hell. They were a little surprised to see each other there. The Presbyterian and charismatic pastor turned to the Methodist and asked why he thought he ended up in hell. "I have always tried to live a perfect life," the Methodist pastor said. "I did until the day before I died, and then I really blew it. I guess that is why I'm here!" He turned to the Presbyterian and asked why he thought he ended up in hell. "I have always believed in divine election and the sovereignty of God," the Presbyterian pastor said. "I guess I wasn't one of the elect!" They turned to the charismatic pastor and asked why he ended up in hell. The pastor said, "I declare by faith that I am not here!"

When we appear before God and look back at our present theology, we will all be a little surprised. Theology is our attempt to systematize truth. Over the years our theology will change, or we are not maturing, but what doesn't change is truth. Wise leaders sense no obligation to defend any particular theological system but let the truth speak for itself. Godly leaders know that character is the primary prerequisite to be an elder or deacon. They will be known for their love. Servant leaders don't lord it over their flock. They prove to be an example of what it means to follow Jesus.

Daily Readings

1. Servant Leadership	Matthew 20:20–28
2. Balance of Power	Deuteronomy 17:14–18:21
3. Purposeful Leadership	Genesis 11:1–9
4. Shared Leadership	Numbers 11:10–30
5. Humble Intercession	Numbers 12:1–13; 14:1–23; 16:1–33

1

Servant Leadership

Matthew 20:20–28

Key Point

Christian leaders are subject to the needs of their followers.

Key Verse

By this everyone will know that you are my disciples, if you love one another.

John 13:35

Secure Christian leaders know who they are in Christ. Insecure leaders try to establish their identity and sense of worth in titles, degrees, and positions of authority and power. Insecure parents promote their children to such attainments. Such was the case when the mother of Zebedee's sons (James and John) approached Jesus. She wanted her children to sit on the right and left side of Christ (see Matthew 20:20–21). The Lord said it was not His to offer, and then He asked if they were prepared to drink from the cup He was about to drink (see verses 22–23). When the other ten disciples heard about this, they became indignant (see verse 24).

When people clamor for power and position, it creates interpersonal problems in organizations. What are the others supposed to do when someone climbs over their backs to get ahead? They neither want those kind of people over them, nor do they want to succumb to the same self-serving tactics. Jesus exhorted His disciples not to be like the Gentiles who exercised their authority and lorded it over others. Instead, they were to be like servants and slaves if they wanted to be great (see Matthew 20:25–26).

There is no position lower than that of a servant or a slave. Christian leaders are not supposed to rely on their position as the basis for their leadership. Christian leadership is not position based; it is character based. Those who aspire to the position of an overseer must show by their character that they are qualified (see 1 Timothy 3 and Titus 1). A person's ability to lead may be somewhat dependent on his or her gifts, talents, intelligence, or personality, but that is not what qualifies that individual to be a Christian leader. Even though some believers may be gifted, talented, intelligent, and personable, they should be immediately disqualified if their character is deficient. Christian leaders should be an example to those under their authority and not lord it over them (see 1 Peter 5:1–4).

Leaders are subject to the needs of those who are under their authority, which is why they should lead them to Christ, who will meet all their needs. When problems arise in a company, church, or home, the mantle falls on the one who is ultimately responsible. Nobody calls the maintenance worker, the custodian, or the child during a crisis. All great leaders should sense the burden of being responsible for those who follow them. Jesus certainly did. He served us by giving His life to meet our greatest need. Jesus had no human position of authority in the religious establishment or the state, and yet "the crowds were amazed at his teaching, because he taught as one who had authority, and not as their teachers of the law" (Matthew 7:28–29). The people recognized His authority because of the quality and conduct of His life.

While Christian leaders are not to appeal to their position or demand loyalty to themselves, those who are under their authority are required to respect their position. "Have confidence in your leaders and submit to their authority, because they keep watch over you as those who must give an account. Do this so that their work will be a joy, not a burden, for that would be of no benefit to you" (Hebrews 13:17).

How do you think James and John felt about their mother at the time? How do you think the other disciples felt about James and John at the time?

How can you tell whether a leader is secure or not?

What does it mean to be a "servant leader"?

What kind of a leader would you like to be?

Even if you have no position of leadership, you are still setting an example for someone. What would you like other people to say about you?

Whereas before He brought little children into their midst and called them to imitate their simplicity and lowliness, now He admonishes them in a sharper way from the opposite direction. "You know that the rulers of the gentiles lord it over them. . . ." Loving the first place is not fitting to us, even though it may be among the nations. Such a passion becomes a tyrant. It continually hinders even great men. . . . "If you want proof that I speak truly, look at what I am doing. Look at what I do and suffer. Let the proof of my teaching be my life." . . . For being king of the powers above, He was willing to become man and submitted Himself to be despised and despitefully treated. And not even with this lowliness was He satisfied, but He even came to die.

John Chrysostom (AD 347–407)

2

Balance of Power

Deuteronomy 17:14–18:21

Key Point

Every organizational structure needs checks and balances because absolute authority corrupts absolutely.

Key Verse

Now the overseer is to be above reproach.

1 Timothy 3:2

In Deuteronomy 17:14–18:21, the Lord sets forth the roles and responsibilities of the prophet, priest, and king. The concept of having checks and balances in government—as well as the idea of having executive, legislative, and judicial branches of government—originated from this text. The prophet brought the law, the priest interpreted it, and the king executed it.

The *king* was roughly parallel to our executive branch of government. The Lord never told the Israelites to have a king, but He anticipated they would ask for one in order to be like other nations (see Deuteronomy 17:14–15). The king had to be chosen from one of the Israelites, and he could not be a foreigner. In the same way, the president of the United States must be a natural-born citizen. The king was not to use his office as a means of personal gain, although Solomon, the third king of Israel, violated every one of these restrictions (see 1 Kings 10:21–11:3). Laws are also in place in the United States to make sure that presidents do not use their office for personal gain. Finally, the king was to keep for himself on a scroll a copy of the law so that he would revere God and follow carefully the word of the Lord. The king was not to interpret the law but only execute the law as interpreted by the priests (see Deuteronomy 17:18–20).

The *priests* represented the judicial branch of government. They could not have an allotment or inheritance with Israel (see Deuteronomy 18:1–2). In other words, they could not have any conflict of interest. In the same way, judges in the judiciary branch of the American government must recuse themselves if a particular case presents a conflict of interest.

The *prophets* were to speak the words of the Lord. They wrote the law. If they spoke presumptuously, they were to be removed. If what they said did not come to pass, they were not to be feared (see Deuteronomy 18:17–22). The prophets were like the legislative branch of government that creates the laws of our land. In a representative form of government, legislators (senators and representatives) are supposed to speak on behalf of the people who put them into office. If they speak presumptuously and fail to represent the people, the people remove them in coming elections.

Only Christ is qualified to be prophet, priest, and king. No person is good enough to rule without checks and balances. Under the New Covenant, we have pastors (pastor-teacher), shepherds (elders), and administrators (overseers). Although the terms "pastor," "elder," and "overseer" refer to the same office, they do not describe the same function. They roughly parallel the roles of prophet (pastor), priest (elder), and king (overseer) and make up the leadership of the local church.

The New Testament teaches a plurality of elders so that one person does not hold all the authority. Christ is the head of the Church, and He alone rules. Elders collectively discern the will of God and lead the people by proclaiming the Word of God, caring for the people, and by overseeing a ministry that ensures every member of the Body of Christ is contributing to the good of all.

What restrictions were placed on the king? What happens if presidents overstep their authority and exert their own will on the people?

What restrictions were placed on the priests? Two-thirds of all laws are presently being established through the judiciary in the United States. What is wrong with that?

What restrictions were placed on the prophets? What happens if elected senators and representatives act presumptuously and fail to represent the people?

Why do we need checks and balances in organizational structures?

What checks and balances do you have in your own life?

_____

_____

_____

"If a man seeks the office of a bishop, he desires a good work."
What is terrible is to desire the absolute authority and power
of the bishop but not the work itself.

John Chrysostom (AD 347–407)

Therefore whoever desires the office of bishop with this un-
derstanding [a good work] wants it without the arrogance of
ambition. To express this more clearly, if a man wants not so
much to be in authority over the people of God as to help them,
he aspires to be a bishop in the true spirit.

Caesarius of Arles (AD 470–542)

3

Purposeful Leadership
Genesis 11:1–9

Key Point

Nothing we purpose to do will be impossible if we have unity among the people, an effective communicative system, a commonly shared objective, and God's blessing.

Key Verses

I pray also for those who will believe in me through their message, that all of them may be one, Father, just as you are in me and I am in you. May they also be in us so that the world may believe that you have sent me.

John 17:20–21

If you know *how* to accomplish a certain task you will likely have a job, but you will work for the one who knows *why* the task is necessary. Why are we here? and Why are we doing what we are doing? are the two most basic questions in life. As Christians, we should have a sense of purpose in life and a reason for doing what we are doing. Our purpose is to glorify God by manifesting His presence in this world and do all to the glory of God. We are to know Him and make Him known by fulfilling the Great Commission. All this is to be done in keeping with the Great Commandment: to love God with all our being and love one another in the same way God has loved us. Do that well, and you will fulfill your purpose.

In the Old Testament, the descendants of Noah decided that they were going to build a tower that reached to heaven. The Lord said, "If as one people speaking the same language they have begun to do this, then nothing they plan to do will be impossible for them" (Genesis 11:6). What did God observe about these people that led Him to make such a statement? These people had three out of the four key ingredients that are essential for the success of any ministry.

First, the people had a common objective. A well-defined purpose or mission statement keeps people moving in the same direction. Second, they had unity. They were one people. Leadership is the ability to unite the church to accomplish a mutually shared objective. When that objective is accomplished, all the members feel satisfied with their contribution. Third, they had an effective communication system. They were one people speaking the same language. Little will be accomplished if the members of a church cannot walk in the light and speak the truth in love with one another.

Let's take a closer look at the importance of communication. Fulfilling our purpose in our homes and churches requires us to keep the lines of communication open. Building consensus requires good communication skills. People need to be heard, not just told. It is hard to get a commitment from people to do our will, but it is easy to get a commitment from others to do their will. People are already committed to doing what they think is right. If they are heard and sense that they have contributed to the plan, they will get behind the leaders and support them. All God had to do to disrupt the peoples' plans to build the tower was destroy their communication system (see Genesis 11:7–9). When they couldn't speak to each other, they scattered.

The fourth ingredient is the desire to do God's will. The Tower of Babel was never completed because the people never consulted God. It was their idea to build a tower and make a name for themselves. So let's learn from their mistake. Let's first collectively discern the will of God to determine a common objective and then establish an effective communication system

88

and unity among the people. Once we have taken these four steps, there is nothing we purpose to do that will be impossible for us.

In Genesis 11:1–9, why did God decide to confuse the people's language?

What three traits did the people possess that are essential for success in ministry?

What kind of leader does it take to unite people around a common objective?

Do you find it easier to do a task yourself or work together with others toward a common objective? Why?

Have you ever seen a good work suffer for lack of communication? How can you strengthen communication in your own life?

To be members one of another points to a great mystery. He is speaking of those who are very close to us in faith. For people are not generally "members one of another." But the faithful indeed are members of the faithful. Christians are members of the body of Christ. We are members with the saints who embody purity of heart and consummate goodness. . . . Hence we are being instructed to speak intimately of the truth of this mystery with the neighbor.

Jerome (AD 347–420)

4

Shared Leadership

Numbers 11:10–30

Key Point

Servant leaders equip the saints to do the work of ministry.

Key Verse

The things you have heard me say in the presence of many witnesses entrust to reliable people who will also be qualified to teach others.

2 Timothy 2:2

Every Christian leader has felt the burden of ministry. Some have felt so inadequate for the task that they wished they were dead. Like Moses, they would rather die than be around for their own demise. No matter how well a pastor preaches and teaches, there will always be some who say, "I'm not getting fed around here." Christian leaders who feel the burden of ministry should keep in mind that the two most powerful Kingdom figures in the Old Testament—Moses and Elijah—both requested to die during their ministry experience (see Numbers 11:15; 1 Kings 19:3–4).

The Lord told Moses, "Bring me seventy of Israel's elders who are known to you as leaders and officials among the people" (Numbers 11:16).

God would take of the Spirit that rested on Moses and put it on them, and they would carry the burden of the people. Jethro gave similar advice to Moses in Exodus 18:17–23. Jethro wasn't suggesting an authoritarian or hierarchical rule. The organizational structure he proposed was designed to relieve Moses' burden, because Moses had been trying to do it all by himself.

Godly leaders are not micromanagers who have to control everything. They are secure in Christ and aren't driven by the need to be needed. They are not worried about job security. They are not hirelings who do all the ministry by themselves, though there are some church members who think they are. They don't have a "Messiah Complex" and think they are the only ones who can do the ministry.

The purpose of Christian leadership is "to equip [God's] people for works of service, so that the body of Christ may be built up until we all reach unity in the faith and in the knowledge of the Son of God and become mature" (Ephesians 4:12–13). There are not enough pastors and professional counselors to help even five percent of the people, even if that is all they did. If we don't see the need to equip the layperson to do the work of ministry, it is not going to get done. It takes the whole Church to "carry each other's burdens, and in this way . . . fulfill the law of Christ" (Galatians 6:2). Professionalism can actually cripple the Church if we believe that only the elite are qualified to help others.

In Numbers 11, when the Spirit rested on the elders they prophesied only once, but Eldad and Medad continued prophesying. Joshua wanted them to stop, but Moses said, "Are you jealous for my sake? I wish that all the LORD's people were prophets and that the LORD would put his Spirit on them!" (verse 29).

As Christian leaders, do we want the Spirit of God to rest on others as He does on us? Do we want the Lord's anointing to be on others as we would have it be on us? Do we get as much delight when others have the spotlight in the kingdom of God as we do when it is our turn? Do we earnestly seek to help all the members of our churches reach their highest potential, even if it means they are able to do some aspects of ministry better than us? Do we rejoice when others bear fruit and get more attention than we do? If we are truly servant leaders, we do.

In Numbers 11:10–30, what did God instruct Moses to do to ease the burden of his leadership?

Why don't all Christian leaders recruit and train other leaders, thus sharing their ministry and helping many more?

How is it possible that a "Christian leader" might actually be the one who is keeping others from reaching their highest potential?

Have you ever felt suppressed by "Christian" leaders? Why do you think that happened? Were you a threat to them, were you trying to usurp their role, or were they trying to control you? Note: such self-analysis will help you know how and where to serve in the future.

How can you multiply yourself by equipping reliable people and delegating responsibility to others?

"You, therefore, my son, be strong in the grace that is in Christ Jesus, and the things you have heard from me in many exhortations, the same you should commit to faithful men, who shall be able to teach others also." The blessed apostle delivered these things with a pious caution, aware that they could be easily known and distorted by anyone who does not have faith. How much greater will be our danger, if, rashly and without thought, we commit the revelations of God to profane and unworthy men.

Hippolytus of Rome (AD 170–235)

5

Humble Intercession

Numbers 12:1–13; 14:1–23; 16:1–33

Key Point

God is looking for servant leaders who humbly intercede for the people they lead, even when they rebel against them.

Key Verse

Humble yourselves, therefore, under God's mighty hand, that he may lift you up in due time.

1 Peter 5:6

oses was the most humble man on the face of the earth (see Numbers 12:3). He demonstrated incredible humility when his staff, congregation, and elders challenged his authority and leadership. First, Moses' sister, Miriam, and brother, Aaron, began to talk against him (see verses 1–2). The Lord called all three out to the Tent of Meeting and spoke to them. The Lord wanted to know why Miriam and Aaron weren't afraid to speak against the one whom He had chosen to lead His people (see verses 5–9). When the Lord departed, Miriam had leprosy (see verse 10). It would be human nature for Moses to be mad at his sibling and welcome God's discipline, but Moses interceded on her behalf and God relented. The leprosy would last only for a week (see verses 11–14).

In Numbers 14:1–4, the entire assembly was discouraged because of the bad report from ten of the spies. They were ready to stone Moses, but then the Lord intervened again (see verse 10). God said He would strike them down with a plague for their unbelief and make Moses into an even greater nation (see verses 11–12). If your congregation was about to stone you and God Himself said He was going to do away with them and give you an even greater ministry, wouldn't you feel just a little bit vindicated— and maybe even excited—about having a bigger ministry? How many of us would pass that test?

Rather than rejoicing, Moses was concerned about God's reputation. What would the pagan nations think if God brought these people out into the wilderness only to destroy them? So Moses prayed that God would withhold His judgment, and God did (see verses 13–20). As with Miriam, the sentence was commuted (see verses 21–23).

In Numbers 16, Moses was tested again. This time, the community leaders who had been appointed members of the council rose up against Moses. Again the Lord intervened, and He said to Moses and Aaron, "Separate yourselves from this assembly so I can put an end to them at once" (Numbers 16:21). How many of us would be making a fast retreat? Moses again cried out to God and said, "O God, the God who gives breath to all living things, will you be angry with the entire assembly when only one man sins?" (Numbers 16:22). Again God relented, and the ground swallowed up only the leaders and their families (see verses 26–33).

If you are a pastor or leader and wonder why God doesn't intervene for you when the people reject your leadership, you may have missed the point. Moses wasn't praying that God would judge those who rebelled against him. He was praying that God would *withhold* judgment. Would your church profit more if you prayed for God's judgment on your staff, board, and congregation, or would they profit more if you prayed that God would withhold His judgment? The Lord said in Ezekiel 22:30, "I looked for someone among them who would build up the wall and stand before me in the gap on behalf of the land so I would not destroy it, but I found no one." God is looking for more servant leaders like Moses.

In Numbers 12:1–13, how did Moses intercede on behalf of Miriam?

In Numbers 14:1–4, what response did Moses give when God said that He was going to do away with the people?

In Numbers 16:1–33, how did Moses seek to again protect the people from God's wrath? How did God respond?

"Do not touch my anointed ones; do my prophets no harm" (Psalm 105:15). If you were a Christian leader, would you quote that psalm in your defense, or is that a warning to those in submissive roles? Explain.

What lessons can you learn from Moses' life about humility and leadership?

_____

_____

_____

After teaching the elders how to preside over the church [1 Peter 5:1], Peter turns his attention to the younger members of the congregation. They are to obey their parents. There is no need for them to do a lot of talking; all that is required is that they show an example of submission. For after teaching the elders how they should treat those under them, it is enough for the younger people to respect the good examples of their elders and imitate them carefully. But in order to avoid a situation in which the higher-ups will think that humility is owed to them by their inferiors but not the other way around, Peter goes on to add that we must all show humility to one another.

Bede (AD 673–735)

Discipleship Counseling

For a long time, I believed my story was unique. I wondered if anyone else in the world endured the types of spiritual conflict I was experiencing. Although I felt alone, I was sure that I couldn't be the only one. My problems had begun a couple years prior. I was experiencing terribly demonic nightmares and even had nights in which I felt the presence of something in my room. One night, I woke feeling like someone was choking me and I could not speak or say the name of Jesus. I was terrified!

I sought help from church leaders and pastors. They had no idea how to encourage me. Eventually fear turned into panic anxiety disorder. My thoughts were so loud, destructive, and frightening that I visited my Christian primary care provider. I thought for sure she would understand my belief that this was a spiritual battle. When I expressed the idea that the enemy was attacking me, she responded by diagnosing me with bipolar disorder and told me I'd have to be on medication for the rest of my life. She also gave me a prescription for anti-depressants and anti-anxiety meds. I was devastated.

I told my husband the diagnosis, and he assured me that it wasn't true. I decided not to take the medication. I just didn't have peace about it. My pastors prayed over me, but nothing changed. I began Christian counseling, which helped a bit, but it was nowhere near worth the $400 per month I paid. When I told my Christian counselor about what was happening in my mind and about my fears, she too said, "I think it's time for medication." It seemed like everyone thought I was crazy. No one believed that my problem was truly spiritual.

Thankfully, I came across the book *Who I Am in Christ* and read stories of people to whom I could relate. I knew there was an answer. It was in that book that I first heard of The Steps to Freedom in Christ. Honestly, I was scared of the Steps at first. I didn't know what to expect. Going through the Steps was one of the most difficult, yet incredible things I've done. I experienced a lot of interference, such as headaches and confusion, but having the Holy Spirit reveal to me all that I needed to renounce was incredible.

When I prayed and asked God to bring to mind the sins of my ancestors, I was shocked at all that came up. I don't even know my ancestors! I later asked my mom about the things that came to mind, and she confirmed that my family line had been involved in all those things. I was amazed at how the Holy Spirit brought out the truth.

After going through the Steps, my mind was completely silent. It was amazing. I remember the pastor asking me to close my eyes and tell him what I was hearing. I paused. I heard only the air conditioning in the room. There were no nagging voices. I was totally at peace. I wanted to cry with joy. After that, I wasn't afraid of being alone. The nightmares were gone. I didn't have to always play the radio or television to drown out terrible thoughts. I could sit in silence and be still, and it was beautiful.

Now a day being alone in the quiet is one of my favorite things to do. I have worked to maintain my freedom, regularly reminding myself of the truth, praying God's Word, and having to forgive new offenses that arise along the way. Now I know that nothing is too difficult for God. The liberating ministry of the Holy Spirit is still active.

—personal testimony shared with the author

Daily Readings

1. Liberated in Christ	Matthew 12:1–50
2. The Truth Encounter	Acts 20:13–38
3. Setting Captives Free	2 Timothy 2:22–26
4. The Wonderful Counselor	Isaiah 61:1–3
5. A Call to Live a Righteous Life	2 Peter 3:1–18

1

Liberated in Christ

Matthew 12:1–50

Key Point

Repentance and faith in God is the only means of resolving personal and spiritual conflicts.

Key Verse

Therefore go and make disciples of all nations.

Matthew 28:19

Matthew 12 presents Jesus as God's chosen servant. He is the Lord of the Sabbath (see verses 1–13) who fulfilled the prophecies of Isaiah and Jonah (see verses 15–21, 38–42). He demonstrated His authority over the kingdom of darkness (see verses 22–32). He considered those who did His Father's will to be spiritually related to Him (see verses 46–50). He also showed wholistic concern for the plight of His people. If they were physically disabled or diseased, He healed them. If His disciples were hungry, He saw that they were fed, even if it violated manmade religious traditions, which He disdained.

The demon-possessed man brought to Jesus in verse 22 was blind and mute, and the Lord healed him physically and spiritually at the same time. Today we try to determine whether somebody's problem is psychological or spiritual, which creates a false dichotomy. Human problems always have a psychological element, because our soul is an integral part of our life, but they always have a spiritual element as well. There is no time when God is not present, and there is no time or place where it would be safe to take off the armor of God. The world is in a mess because of the Fall, and Jesus has only one answer: "Repent and believe the good news" (Mark 1:15). Christian ministry is an encounter with God. He affects the whole person and incorporates all reality all the time.

Suppose your life is like a house and you haven't taken out the garbage or cleaned up any spills for six months. That will attract a lot of flies, which you would really like to get rid of. Would it help to study the flight patterns of all the flies and determine their names and rank? You could exercise authority over them and demand that they leave, but they would likely come back and find the house empty. They also may tell seven others where the garbage is, which would result in even greater bondage (Matthew 12:45). The goal is to get rid of the garbage. Repentance and faith in God have been and will continue to be the answer until Christ returns, whether the problem is primarily psychological or primarily spiritual. Submitting to God without resisting the devil could leave someone in bondage. Trying to resist the devil without first submitting to God will prove futile.

Jesus confronted demons, but He didn't get into any dialogue with them. If we dialogue with demons in another person, we are bypassing the victim, who needs to repent and choose the truth. If we dialogue with demons and believe what they say, we will be deceived, because they all speak from their own nature and are all liars (see John 8:44). The Steps to Freedom in Christ is a repentance process that is an encounter with God that doesn't allow any demons to manifest. It is a ministry of reconciliation that removes the barriers to one's intimacy with God.

The Church has been commissioned to continue Christ's ministry of setting captives free and binding up the brokenhearted. To be an effective instrument in His hand, we must be liberated in Christ ourselves and be totally dependent on Him, for apart from Christ we can do nothing.

In Matthew 12, how did Jesus demonstrate that He was the long-awaited Messiah?

What is wrong with ministering to a person only psychologically or only spiritually?

The glory of God is a manifestation of His presence. So what is wrong with letting demons manifest?

Jesus said Satan is the ruler of this world, and Paul said we wrestle not with flesh and blood but spiritual forces. How do you feel about that statement?

What confidence did you get from reading Matthew 12?

_____

_____

_____

To cast out demons is a work of the highest power and not of any ordinary power. For Matthew said, "If it is by the Spirit of God that I cast out demons," just as Luke said, "If I by the finger of God cast out demons." The inference then might seem to be that if this is so, then quite obviously the Son of God has appeared. . . . He dimly intimates it by saying, "Then the kingdom of God has come upon you." Do you grasp this wisdom? His presence was quietly shining forth precisely through the very things to which they were assigning blame.

John Chrysostom (AD 347–407)

2

The Truth Encounter

Acts 20:13–38

Key Point

All the darkness of the world cannot withstand the light of one candle.

Key Verses

If you hold to my [Jesus'] teaching, you are really my disciples. Then you will know the truth, and the truth will set you free.

John 8:31–32

Paul was an exemplary role model for the elders at Ephesus in Acts 20:13–38, where he called for repentance and faith in Jesus Christ. He warned them that spiritual wolves would arise from their own numbers and distort the truth. Without genuine repentance there will be spiritual problems within the church. Outside the church is much worse. "The whole world is under the control of the evil one" (1 John 5:19) because Satan "leads the whole world astray" (Revelation 12:9).

Repentance literally means a change of mind, and to have faith in Jesus means to believe the truth. Obviously, the battle is for the mind. Spiritual warfare is better understood as a truth encounter rather than a power encounter. We are not caught in a battle between two equal powers but opposite powers. Jesus clearly demonstrated His superiority over the forces of evil. It is a battle between the Spirit of Truth and the father of lies.

There are no biblical instructions to pursue power because we already have all the power we need to live a righteous life and minister to others (see Ephesians 1:18–19). Satan has been disarmed (see Colossians 2:15), and the only way he continues to rule is through deception. When his lies are exposed, his pretense of power is broken.

Before the cross, Satan had not been disarmed and God's people had not been redeemed. So it took some specially endowed authority agent to expel demons, which is why Jesus gave His disciples "power and authority to drive out all demons" (Luke 9:1). Jesus also gave special authority and power to the seventy-two appointees in the next chapter (see Luke 10:17). After Pentecost, every believer has the same power and authority to do God's will, which is why there are no instructions in the Epistles for casting out demons within the Church. It is no longer the outside agent's responsibility. The deliverer is Christ, and He has already come.

We don't get our information from deceiving spirits. The Holy Spirit, who is the Spirit of Truth, leads us into all truth, and that truth will set us free. No outside agent can repent for us or believe for us. That is a choice we all have to make in order to experience our freedom in Christ. The only power that Satan has is the power we give him through fear and unbelief. He controls people through lies and intimidation.

A family was riding in their car when a bee flew through a window. The children in the back seat started to panic. "Daddy, there's a bee in the car!" The father calmly reached back and grasped the bee in his hand. The children didn't see the bee's stinger pierce the father's hand and deposit its poison. Then the father released the bee, and the children started to panic again until the father showed them the stinger in his hand. The bee had been disarmed. Jesus said, "Why are you troubled, and why do doubts rise in your minds? Look at my hands and my feet" (Luke 24:38–39). Jesus was saying, "I took the stinger." Then Jesus said, "Because you have seen me, you have believed; blessed are those who have not seen and yet have believed" (John 20:29).

What warning did Paul give the Ephesian elders in Acts 20:28–31?

What kinds of problems will likely plague the church if professing Christians haven't repented and are still believing lies?

Why is spiritual warfare more a truth encounter than a power encounter?

Since beginning this study, how have you changed your mind about God, yourself, and Satan?

Whom do you fear the most—God or Satan? Why?

The "world"—that is, those who love the world—are subjected to evil. This includes everybody, because we are all born under sin, which traces its origin to the disobedience of Adam. . . . The word refers to people, not to the material substance of creation.

Didymus the Blind (AD 313–398)

3

Setting Captives Free

2 Timothy 2:22–26

Key Point

We must depend on God, because He is the One who grants forgiveness.

Key Verse

They will come to their senses and escape from the trap of the devil, who has taken them captive to do his will.

2 Timothy 2:26

The ministries of discipleship and counseling are essentially the same in Scripture. A godly counselor is also a good discipler and vice versa. Discipleship counselors know that God is always present during ministry times and that there is a role only He can fulfill. In 2 Timothy 2:22–26, Paul provides a pastoral model for helping others experience their freedom in Christ through genuine repentance and faith in God.

First, *the discipling counselor is the Lord's servant*. Discipleship counseling is an encounter with God. Discipleship counselors are dependent on God. They know that only God can set a captive free and bind up the brokenhearted.

Second, *discipleship counselors are not quarrelsome*. The goal is not to win the argument but to avoid it. You have lost control if the ministry session has degenerated into a quarrel. You can't help somebody who is not cooperative or doesn't want to get well, because what lasts is not what the encourager does but what the inquirer does.

Third, *discipleship counselors are kind to all*. Jesus said, "Go and learn what this means: 'I desire mercy, not sacrifice'" (Matthew 9:13). Mercy comes from the Hebrew word *hesed*, which is translated in the Old Testament as "lovingkindness" (NASB) or "compassion." We are working with wounded people who cannot handle harsh treatment, criticism, or rejection. They need to tell us their story, but they won't do so if we aren't the kind of people with whom they feel safe to share it.

Fourth, *discipleship counselors are able to teach*. That means we must know the truth that will set people free. People are not in bondage to past traumas; they are in bondage to the lies they have believed because of the trauma. They have no interest in sharing their problems just for the purpose of sharing them with another individual, but they will share their deepest secrets with God for the purpose of resolving their problems.

Fifth, *discipleship counselors are not resentful—they are "patient when wronged"* (2 Timothy 2:24 NASB). We can't bring our own problems into the counseling session and expect to help someone else. We have to be free in Christ ourselves in order to be used by God to set others free. It takes great patience to work with wounded captives.

Sixth, *discipleship counselors are gentle like Jesus*. The only time the Lord ever described Himself was in Matthew 11:29: "I am gentle and humble in heart." We cannot run roughshod over people, move too fast, or get ahead of God's timing. Patience is a virtue. Have you noticed that those who never have enough time to do it right the first time have enough time to do it over again?

Paul is not presenting a confrontational "power encounter" but a kind, compassionate, and able-to-teach model. He starts by saying we must be dependent on God, and he ends with God being the One who grants repentance that leads to a knowledge of the truth. Truth is what sets the captives free. The phrase "they may come to their senses" (2 Timothy 2:26) reveals where the battle is waging. (The book *Discipleship Counseling* and The Steps to Freedom in Christ are based on this model.)

Why must the discipleship counselor be dependent on God?

_____

_____

_____

Why is it necessary to be gentle and kind?

_____

_____

_____

What is wrong with quarreling?

_____

_____

_____

Do you think Paul is presenting a professional model of counseling or a godly approach to ministry? How are they different?

_____

_____

_____

_____

Do you personally believe that repentance and faith in God are an adequate answer for people who have psychological and spiritual problems? Why or why not?

Therefore, let us not be provoked with these men, let us not use anger as an excuse, but let us talk with them gently and with kindness. Nothing is more forceful and effective than treatment which is gentle and kind. . . . He [the shepherd] needs therefore a heroic spirit, not to grow despondent or neglect the salvation of wanderers but to keep on thinking and saying, "God perhaps may give the knowledge of the truth, and they may be freed from the snare of the devil."

John Chrysostom (AD 347–407)

4

The Wonderful Counselor

Isaiah 61:1–3

Key Point

God is present in every ministry, and defining who is responsible for what will determine how successful we are.

Key Verse

He heals the brokenhearted and binds up their wounds.

Psalm 147:3

Jesus quoted the first part of this passage in Isaiah when He stood up in a synagogue to read from God's Word on the Sabbath (see Luke 4:14–22). Jesus stopped reading in the middle of Isaiah 61:2 after the word "favor," emphasizing what He would accomplish in His first advent. When He comes again, He will fulfill verses 2 and 3. Judgment will come for unbelievers, but a garment of praise will come for those who trust in Him.

During this Church Age, God has committed Himself to working through His children as they minister one to another. So when we minister to the spiritual captive and the brokenhearted, we can be assured that Jesus is present and that He wants to set them free and bind up their broken hearts. Discipleship counselors are encouragers who acknowledge God's presence and recognize that apart from Christ, they can do nothing.

Discipleship counseling is the process of building the life of Christ into one another. It is a relational experience centered on the Word of God in the presence of Christ and one another. Think of the setting as a triangle:

Every side of the triangle represents a relationship. For discipleship counselors, the most important relationship is the one they have with God. They cannot impart to others what they themselves do not possess. It is also important how the encourager relates to the inquirer. Sadly, that is the only relationship that is considered in secular counseling.

Now ask yourself the question *Who is responsible for what*? Have you ever usurped God's role and tried to play the role of the Holy Spirit in your spouse's life? In an inquirer's life? How well did that work? Have you ever tried to assume the responsibility of the one you were trying to help? How well did that work? Can you really help inquirers who won't assume responsibility for their own attitudes and actions? Can you forgive others for them? Can you believe for them? Can you think for them? Can you repent for them?

What are we actually trying to accomplish in the above diagram? We are trying to help inquirers establish a righteous relationship with God. It is a ministry of reconciliation that cannot happen without the presence of the wonderful Counselor. He is the one who grants repentance. He is the One who will convict them of their sin. He is the One who knows every minute detail of the inquirers' lives, who just happen to be His children.

The encourager takes the time to listen to the inquirer's story and then asks, "Would you like to resolve these issues?" Nobody ever says no. After that commitment, the encourager says, "With your permission, I will lead you through these Steps to Freedom. If anything good happens today, it is because of what you choose to believe and do. We will be looking at several issues that may be affecting your relationship with God. We will start each step by having you pray, asking your heavenly Father to reveal to your mind what issues are keeping you from having an intimate relationship with Him. He is the One who will grant you repentance and set you free."

Why do you think Jesus read from Isaiah 61:1–3?

_____

_____

_____

Why is it so important to know who is responsible for what?

_____

_____

_____

How does discipleship counseling differ from professional counseling?

_____

_____

_____

Do you react differently when God convicts you of sin as opposed to someone else pointing out your sin? Why?

_____

_____

_____

We worship God to keep His divine attributes clearly embedded in our minds. Why have so many church "ministries" functioned as though God isn't even present?

The Lord told us, "Outside of Me you can do nothing." This is because our weakness, when moved to do good things, is unable to bring anything to completion without the Giver of good things. The one who has come to understand the weakness of human nature has had experience of the divine power. And such a person who because of divine power has succeeded in some things and is eager to succeed in others never looks down on anyone. For he knows that in the same way that God has helped him and freed him from many passions and hardships, so can he help everyone when He wishes, especially those who are striving for His sake.

Maximus the Confessor (AD 580–662)

5

A Call to Live
a Righteous Life

2 Peter 3:1–18

Key Point

Plan to live for many years, but live as though the Lord may return tomorrow.

Key Verse

He will send his angels with a loud trumpet call, and they will gather his elect from the four winds, from one end of the heavens to the other.

Matthew 24:31

We don't know the day or the hour, but we do know that the Lord is coming again. In the Olivet Discourse in Matthew 24, Jesus gives us the signs of the end of the age. He warns us not to be deceived, because there will be false Christs and false prophets, and there will be a coming apostasy before He returns. Peter said there would be scoffers who make fun of the Second Advent (see 2 Peter 3:2–4).

In our modern age—with its wars and rumors of wars, earthquakes and famine, and increasing lawlessness—many of us ask why the Lord doesn't come back now. The reason is because He looks into the kingdom of darkness and sees millions who have never heard the gospel. If He were to shut the door now, how many of our friends, relatives, neighbors, and co-workers would be shut out of His kingdom for all eternity? He is waiting for "this gospel of the kingdom [to be] preached in the whole world as a testimony to all nations, and then the end will come" (Matthew 24:14). "The Lord is not slow in keeping his promise, as some understand slowness. Instead he is patient with you, not wanting anyone to perish, but everyone to come to repentance" (2 Peter 3:9).

Listen to some of Paul's final words: "In the presence of God and of Christ Jesus, who will judge the living and the dead, and in view of his appearing and his kingdom, I give you this charge: Preach the word; be prepared in season and out of season; correct, rebuke, and encourage—with great patience and careful instruction. For the time will come when people will not put up with sound doctrine. Instead, to suit their own desires, they will gather around them a great number of teachers to say what their itching ears want to hear. They will turn their ears away from the truth and turn aside to myths. But you, keep your head in all situations, endure hardship, do the work of an evangelist, discharge all the duties of your ministry" (2 Timothy 4:1–5).

The only way to hasten the day of the Lord is to do the work of an evangelist, which you should do out of love for God and others anyway. "The day of the Lord will come like a thief" (2 Peter 3:10), when you least expect it. Jesus could come tomorrow or next year or next century. So the real question is what kind of person you ought to be. Peter said, "You ought to live holy and godly lives as you look forward to the day of God and speed its coming" (verses 11–12).

May the good Lord bless you and encourage you as you seek to be all that God has created you to be. "To him who is able to keep you from stumbling and to present you before his glorious presence without fault and with great joy—to the only God our Savior be glory, majesty, power and authority, through Jesus Christ our Lord, before all ages, now and forevermore" (Jude 1:24–25).

Paul says there will be a falling away from God before the Second Coming (see 2 Thessalonians 2:1–10), and Jesus said there would be difficult days ahead. How should we prepare for that?

_____

_____

_____

Paul says in 2 Timothy 4:1–5 that people will not endure sound doctrine. What evidence do you see of that happening today?

_____

_____

_____

How does the Bible instruct us to live as we wait for the Second Advent?

_____

_____

_____

Are you living as if Jesus could return at any time? Why or why not?

_____

_____

_____

Why do you think God hasn't revealed the day or hour of Christ's return?

Peter is talking about those holy vigils [2 Peter 3:14], which Jesus referred to when He said: "Blessed are those servants whom the Master finds awake when He comes" [Luke 12:37]. The person who keeps himself pure from evil may be said to be watching, as may the one who does his utmost to live in peace with everyone.

Bede (AD 673–735)

The Divine Perspective

In 2 Kings 6, the king of Aram was at war with Israel, but his plans were always thwarted because Elisha would send a word of warning to the king of Israel. The king of Aram thought there was a traitor among them, but one of his officers said, "Elisha, the prophet who is in Israel, tells the king of Israel the very words you speak in your bedroom" (verse 12). Hearing this, the king of Aram sent an army to capture Elisha and surrounded the city where he was staying.

When the servant of the man of God got up and went out early the next morning, an army with horses and chariots had surrounded the city. "Oh no, my lord! What shall we do?" the servant asked. "Don't be afraid," the prophet answered. "Those who are with us are more than those who are with them." And Elisha prayed, "Open his eyes, Lord, so that he may see." Then the Lord opened the servant's eyes, and he looked and saw the hills full of horses and chariots of fire all around Elisha.

verses 15–17

Wisdom is seeing life from God's spiritual and eternal perspective, which is different from our temporal and natural perspective. Paul wrote, "For our light and momentary troubles are achieving for us an eternal glory that far outweighs them all. So we fix our eyes not on what is seen, but on what is unseen. For what is seen is temporary, but what is unseen is eternal" (2 Corinthians 4:17–18). What is unseen is not verifiable through empirical research, which is the gold standard for higher education in the West. We need the Word of God to see with the eyes of faith. The Bible is authoritative, whereas nature is illustrative. Without God's perspective, we have no recourse but to fall back on philosophical speculation and scientific rationalism. Research reveals *what is* verifiable in the natural realm, but it can't explain *why it is*.

Scientific research cannot validate or invalidate the reality of the spiritual world or offer any explanation. God doesn't submit to our methods of investigation, and rest assured that the devil is not going to cooperate with secular research. Satan operates under the cloak of deception and will not voluntarily reveal himself for our benefit. The rational process of verification is always interpreted through the grid of our own cultural, educational, and personal perspectives. Two people can look at the same data and draw completely different conclusions. That is why we must learn to interpret what we see through the grid of Scripture. If we don't have God's perspective, we will have no idea what is happening around us at this present time.

The Kingdom of God

The Western world sees reality in two tiers. The upper tier is the transcendental world where God, ghosts, and ghouls reside—a world that is understood through religion and mysticism. The lower tier is the empirical world that is understood through science and the physical senses. In two-tier mentality, the spiritual world has no or little practical bearing on the natural world. Secular educational systems don't consider it a part of their reality. Humanists and atheists reject the idea of an upper tier.

In stark contrast to Western rationalism and naturalism, other nations of the world have a very different view of reality. They have only one tier. The spiritual world is an integral part of their culture and worldview. Spiritism is the dominant religious orientation in the world, although it is not an organized religion like Judaism, Islam, and Christianity. Westerners dismiss spiritism and animism as inferior worldviews on the basis of our advanced technological and economic success.

Why, then, does the United States have the highest crime rate of any industrial nation in the world? Why is it the greatest distributor of pornographic filth? Why do some nations call the United States "the great Satan"? Neither naturalists nor spiritists have a biblical worldview. The devil doesn't care which one you are, because both are in error and leave you vulnerable to Satan's schemes.

Daily Readings

1. Worldview	Daniel 10:1–21
2. The Kingdom of God	Acts 28:17–31
3. Kingdom Parables	Matthew 13:1–43
4. The Return of Jesus	Zechariah 14:1–9
5. Good Versus Evil	Esther 3:1–15

1

Worldview

Daniel 10:1–21

Key Point

What is seen is temporal and passing away; what is unseen is eternal.

Key Verse

For we live by faith, not by sight.

2 Corinthians 5:7

Worldview is what we believe about the world around us. It consists of the conscious and subconscious suppositions that we hold about reality. Our worldview is shaped by the culture in which we were raised. If our moms and dads read the Bible and prayed about things that mattered, we likely grew up thinking that God was present in our everyday experience.

If we attended a public school, we were taught from a secular perspective, and chances are that the Christian foundation of our Constitution and country, as well as the Great Awakening, weren't taught as a part of

American history. If we watched television, we witnessed almost every aspect of the human drama lived out as though there was no God. As the United States culture becomes increasingly secular, any reference made to the spiritual world is usually a caricature of the real thing. This trend cannot help but influence what our children believe about the world in which they live.

From a biblical worldview, there are three enemies to our sanctification: the world, the flesh, and the devil. We not only live in a fallen world that shaped our old nature (flesh), but we also live in a world that is dominated by spiritual forces that are actively opposing the will of God. Satan is "the prince [ruler] of this world" (John 16:11), "the god of this age" (2 Corinthians 4:4), and "the ruler of the kingdom of the air" (Ephesians 2:2). Satan "leads the whole world astray" (Revelation 12:9), and "the whole world is under the control of the evil one" (1 John 5:19).

Everywhere you look there is immorality, injustice, and bondage to sin. Can that be explained on the basis of sociology, psychology, psychiatry, or politics run amuck, or is that the kingdom of darkness at work? Paul was arguing for the latter when he wrote, "Our struggle is not against flesh and blood, but against the rulers, against the authorities, against the powers of this dark world and against the spiritual forces of evil in the heavenly realms" (Ephesians 6:12). The Son of God appeared "to destroy the devil's work" (1 John 3:8).

This opposition from the kingdom of darkness to the will of God is illustrated in Daniel 10. Daniel prays, fasts, and mourns for three weeks on behalf of Israel's captivity (see verses 2–3). Finally, an angel comes to tell Daniel that his prayers have been heard because of his humility and his desire to gain understanding. The angel said he would have come sooner, "but the prince of the Persian kingdom resisted me twenty-one days. Then Michael, one of the chief princes, came to help me, because I was detained there with the king of Persia" (verse 13). Conservative scholars agree that the "prince of the Persian kingdom" was a spiritual enemy of God who was opposing the Lord's plan to work with Daniel. There is a fierce battle going on in the heavenlies—the spiritual realm—and it is affecting what is happening in the natural realm.

Satan's opposition to the kingdom of God continues to this day, and may actually intensify as the day of the Lord draws near. "The Spirit clearly says that in later times some will abandon the faith and follow deceiving spirits and things taught by demons" (1 Timothy 4:1). That is presently happening all over the world.

How do we develop a worldview?

How can we protect ourselves and our children from being influenced by Western rationalism and naturalism?

What insights do we find in Daniel 10:1–21 as to how the devil operates to oppose God's will? What kind of battle is being waged in the heavenlies right now?

Who or what has influenced your worldview the most? Why?

What do you believe about the world around you?

Why does he call the devil the ruler of this world [John 16:11]? Because virtually the whole of humanity surrendered to him. All are his voluntary and willing slaves. Few pay any heed to Christ, who promises unnumbered blessings. Rather they follow after the devil who promises nothing but leads them all to hell. He rules in this age, where he has . . . more subjects than God, more who obey him than God. All but a few are in his grasp on account of their laxity.

John Chrysostom (AD 347–407)

The Kingdom of God

Acts 28:17–31

Key Point

The Church has been commissioned to expand God's kingdom on earth while He reigns supreme in our hearts.

Key Verses

Our Father in heaven, hallowed be your name, your kingdom come, your will be done, on earth as it is in heaven.

Matthew 6:9–10

Kingdoms have a ruler, a realm, and a reign. God (Ruler) created Adam and Eve to multiply and fill the earth (realm), and they were to rule (reign) over the birds of the sky, the beasts of the field, and the fish of the sea (see Genesis 1:28–30). However, Satan deceived Eve, and Adam sinned (see Genesis 3:6). From that point forward, Satan became the rebel holder of authority—the prince of this world.

Satan rules through his hierarchy of demons, who blind the minds of the unbelieving (see 2 Corinthians 4:4) and deceive and lead astray the hearts and minds of humankind. Satan is portrayed as possessing all the kingdoms of this world (see Luke 4:6). When the devil offered Jesus the kingdoms of this world in exchange for His worship, Jesus never corrected his claim—nor did He succumb to the temptation.

Scripture clearly presents God as the King of kings and Lord of lords of the universe. God sits on His throne (see Ezekiel 1:26–28), where He is surrounded by the heavenly host who serve Him (see 1 Kings 22:19). He watches over the whole earth (see Psalm 33:13). His is the eternal Kingdom (see Psalm 145:13), which overcomes the forces of chaos and disorder symbolized by the flood and the sea (see Psalms 29:10; 93:1–4). His reign is characterized by power and glory (see Psalm 145:11), but also by truth and righteousness (see Psalm 96:13). God alone is the judge of this world (see Psalm 96:10).

In the New Testament, the apostles expected that the kingdom of God would be established through the nation of Israel (see Acts 1:6). John the Baptist, Jesus, and the apostles announced to Israel that the Kingdom was at hand. Did Jesus intend to become the king of Israel and fully establish an earthly kingdom, or did He come to establish His Church and rule in the hearts and minds of His children?

The Protestant church has had three major views about the millennial reign mentioned in Revelation 20. Amillennialists believe there is no future millennium to come. The events in Revelation occur during the Church Age, the gospel will be preached to all the nations, and then Christ will return. Postmillennialists believe the growth of the Church will gradually increase and usher in a reign of peace for a thousand years, and then Christ will return. Premillennialists believe there is a coming apostasy culminating with seven years of tribulation, after which the Lord will return and reign on earth for a thousand years.

Here is what we do know for sure. Satan is the prince of this world, but he has been judged and now stands condemned (see John 16:11). God is the supreme Ruler of the universe, and His children have the authority and power to do His will. We are commissioned to make disciples and carry on the ministry of our Lord by setting captives free and binding up the wounds of the brokenhearted: "And this gospel of the kingdom will be preached in the whole world as a testimony to all nations, and then the end will come" (Matthew 24:14). Satan knows his end is coming, and he will do all he can to impede the progress of the gospel.

Can you identify the ruler, the realm, and the reign in the kingdom of darkness? Explain.

_____

_____

_____

Can two sovereigns be ruling in the same realm at the same time? Who chooses?

_____

_____

_____

What is "the kingdom of God"? How will it be expanded? Will God's kingdom be fully established on the earth?

_____

_____

_____

If you are not choosing God as the king of your life, then who is your king? Do you believe that every person is currently serving in one kingdom or the other? Why or why not?

_____

_____

_____

Why do you think the people rejected Jesus as the King of the Jews?

The Word rules over no one against that person's will. For there are still wicked beings—not only men, but also angels and all demons—over whom we say in a sense He does not rule. For they do not yield Him a willing obedience. However, in another sense of the word, He rules even over them—in the same way as we say that man rules over irrational animals. In other words, He does not rule them by persuasion, but as one who tames and subdues lions and beasts of burden. Nevertheless, He leaves no means untried to persuade even those who are still disobedient to submit to His authority.

Origen (AD 184–253)

3

Kingdom Parables

Matthew 13:1–43

Key Point

Wherever and whenever God sows good seed, the devil sows bad seed.

Key Verses

When Jesus had called the Twelve together, he gave them power and authority to drive out all demons and to cure diseases, and he sent them out to proclaim the kingdom of God and to heal the sick.

Luke 9:1–2

Jesus often used parables to teach Kingdom truths. Parables are illustrative stories drawn from nature and life. When the disciples asked Jesus why He spoke in parables, He replied, "Because the knowledge of the secrets of the kingdom of heaven has been given to you, but not to them" (Matthew 13:11). Paul also said that the natural person cannot discern the things of God (see 1 Corinthians 2:14).

In the parable of the sower, the seed is sown on four different kinds of ground, but only one bears fruit (see Matthew 13:18–23). The devil snatches the message away from some, while others hear the good news but it doesn't take root. Still others are carried away by "the worries of this life and the deceitfulness of wealth" (verse 22). The good soil represents those who hear the Word and understand it. Only the latter bears fruit, which is the evidence that they have new life in Christ.

The parable of the weeds (see Matthew 13:24–30) reveals another truth about the kingdom of heaven. Whenever and wherever God sows a good seed, the devil sows a bad seed. "The field is the world, and the good seed stands for the people of the kingdom. The weeds are the people of the evil one, and the enemy who sows them is the devil" (Matthew 13:37–39). It is unlikely that such weeds are redeemable.

The bad seed (tares or darnel, a poisonous grass) is almost indistinguishable from wheat when the two are in early stages of growth, which is why they weren't separated until harvest time. Which ones they are will be clearly evident at harvest time. Wheat starts out looking like grass but the fruit becomes evident as it matures, while the tares bear no fruit. The wheat multiplies by spreading seed, while the tares propagate underground in the cloak of darkness. The wheat and the tares will coexist until the final harvest, when Jesus sends His angels to weed out His kingdom. The non-fruit-bearing grass will be burned (see verses 40–42).

The good news of the Kingdom is being preached (see Luke 16:16) and our Father is pleased to give us the Kingdom (see Luke 12:32). The present world is under the rule of Satan, but Jesus came to undo the works of Satan (see 1 John 3:8), bring an end to his rule, and liberate those who have been held captive to do his will. The Kingdom is associated with preaching (see Luke 9:2), with spiritual authority over demons (see Mark 1:39; 3:14–15), and with healing (see Luke 9:1–2, 6, 11; 10:9).

After Peter confessed that Jesus was "the Messiah, the Son of the living God" (Matthew 16:16), Jesus said, "On this rock I will build my church, and the gates of Hades will not overcome it. I will give you the keys of the kingdom of heaven" (verses 18–19). What these "keys" of the Kingdom are may be answered in Luke 11:52: "Woe to you experts in the law, because you have taken away the key to knowledge. You yourselves have not entered, and you have hindered those who were entering." The "key" is the Truth, the Word who became flesh, the Door to eternity. Jesus said, "No one comes to the Father except through me" (John 14:6).

Why did Jesus teach the people by using parables?

_____

_____

_____

In the parable of the sower in Matthew 13:18–23, only one soil bore any fruit. What conclusions should we draw from that?

_____

_____

_____

_____

In the parable of the weeds in Matthew 13:24–30, who are the wheat and who are the tares? How does each propagate? What conclusions should we draw from that?

_____

_____

_____

_____

If you are a true believer, how would the world know that (see Matthew 7:16)?

_____

_____

_____

Why do you think Jesus warned His disciples not to tell others who He was?

....

....

....

"Let both grow together until harvest" seems to be contrary to the other precept: "Put away evil from your midst." . . . Between wheat and weeds there is something called darnel, when the plant is in its early growth. . . . It looks like an ear of corn [wheat], and the difference between them is hardly noticeable. The Lord therefore advises us that we should not be quick to judge what is doubtful but should leave judgment up to God. So when the Day of Judgment comes, He may not cast out from the body of saints those who are suspected of misdeeds but those who are obviously guilty. As to His words that the bundles of weeds are to be consigned to the fire and the wheat to be gathered in the barn, it is clear that all heretics and hypocrites are to be burned in the fires of hell. But the holy ones, who are called wheat, are to be gathered up in barns—that is to say, heavenly mansions.

Jerome (AD 347–420)

4

The Return of Jesus
Zechariah 14:1–9

Key Point

The eternal purpose of God was to make His manifold wisdom known through the Church to the rulers and authorities in the heavenly realm.

Key Verse

For the Lord himself will come down from heaven, with a loud command, with the voice of the archangel and with the trumpet call of God, and the dead in Christ will rise first.

1 Thessalonians 4:16

Zechariah prophesied that the Lord would one day "be king over the whole earth" (Zechariah 14:9). The coming of the Kingdom is a recurring theme in Scripture. Although the Kingdom was present in the ministry of Jesus, He also spoke of it as being in the future. He told His disciples to pray for its coming (see Matthew 6:10) and to be ready when it comes (see Matthew 25:1–13). When Jesus said a number of times that it was coming soon (see Matthew 16:28; Mark 9:1), He was referring to the age yet to come (see Mark 10:30). The future Kingdom was associated with the Second Coming of Jesus, the resurrection of the dead, and the setting up of an eternal peace in His presence. It is described as a feast (see Matthew 8:11) or wedding feast (see Matthew 22:2).

If the presence of the Kingdom is closely associated with Jesus, then its future coming must be associated with His Second Coming. The two events form a single future hope. Even though the future Kingdom is imminent for us, Jesus indicated there would be an interval between His death and its arrival. During this time, His disciples were given the keys to the kingdom (see Matthew 16:19) and were instructed to preach the gospel to all the nations (see Matthew 24:14). The Church Age was a "mystery," which means that its existence had not been previously revealed.

In Ephesians 3:8–11, Paul tells us the purpose of the Church: "This grace was given me: to preach to the Gentiles the boundless riches of Christ, and to make plain to everyone the administration of this mystery, which for ages past was kept hidden in God, who created all things. His intent was that now, through the church, the manifold wisdom of God should be made known to the rulers and authorities in the heavenly realms, according to his eternal purpose that he accomplished in Christ Jesus our Lord."

According to these words from Paul, the rulers and authorities are in the spiritual realm (the "heavenly realm"), not the natural realm. The Church triumphs over the kingdom of darkness when the children of God lead righteous lives and speak the truth in love. They can do so because Jesus is the head of the Church. "God placed all things under [Jesus'] feet and appointed him to be head over everything for the church, which is his body, the fullness of him who fills everything in every way" (Ephesians 1:22–23).

We don't know when the Lord will come again. "But the day of the Lord will come like a thief. The heavens will disappear with a roar; the elements will be destroyed by fire, and the earth and everything done in it will be laid bare. Since everything will be destroyed in this way, what kind of people ought you to be? You ought to live holy and godly lives as you look forward to the day of God and speed its coming. That day will bring about the destruction of the heavens by fire, and the elements will melt in the heat" (2 Peter 3:10–12). We should make plans to live long, productive lives on earth, but we should live righteously as though Jesus were coming tomorrow.

If the Church was a mystery not yet revealed, how could the nation of Israel know that there would be a gap between the first and second coming of the Messiah?

It is the eternal purpose of God to make His wisdom known through the Church. To whom is this wisdom being taught? How well do you think we are accomplishing His eternal purpose?

Being the Church, what are we commissioned to do?

What do you believe is your primary role in fulfilling God's purpose?

How should you live, knowing the Lord may come like a thief in the night?

His expression through the church means through all the members of God and through every soul that has put on his mysteries and has hope in Him. From this we understand what has been given to humanity. The powers and principalities in heaven are learning the wisdom of God through a human mediator.

Gaius Marius Victorinus (c. fourth century AD)

5

Good Versus Evil

Esther 3:1–15

Key Point

The primary battle on earth is between the kingdom of God and the kingdom of darkness.

Key Verses

We know that we are children of God, and that the whole world is under the control of the evil one.

1 John 5:19

There are no religious references in the book of Esther. God is never mentioned, nor is prayer, worship, or sacrifice. However, the book of Esther clearly illustrates the eternal battle between good and evil. In the normal course of human events, Satan works to destroy God's plan of redemption. However, God controls and directs all the seemingly insignificant coincidences that result in deliverance for His Chosen People.

The events taking place in the Persian city of Susa threatened the continuity of God's plan in redemptive history. Had Haman successfully destroyed all of Mordecai's people (the Jews), it would have prevented the coming of the Messiah (see Esther 3:6). Devout Jews to this day celebrate the Feast of Purim to commemorate the deliverance of the Israelites in Persia (see Esther 9:26–28).

Think of all the times that the Messianic bloodline was threatened. Cain killed Abel, but Eve was granted another son to carry on the family line (see Genesis 4:17). A scapegoat was provided minutes before Abraham sacrificed his son Isaac (see Genesis 22:10–13). A caravan happened to come along when Joseph had been left to die (see Genesis 37:26–28). Moses was spared when all the male Hebrew children were killed (see Exodus 2:1–10). The demonized Saul tried to kill David (see 1 Samuel 19:9–10). Haman tried to annihilate the Jews (see Esther 3:6). Herod ordered all newborn male babies to be killed, which would have included Jesus, but God warned Joseph in a dream to flee to Egypt (see Matthew 2:13–18). Wars, diseases, and natural disasters have threatened God's people, but God has always ensured that there would be a remnant.

History tells us that the Jews were dispersed after the destruction of Jerusalem in AD 70. Throughout the Church Era, they have continued to be persecuted. Had Adolf Hitler been successful during World War II, he would have annihilated the Jews. It is a miracle that the Jewish people have managed to maintain their identity and have reestablished their home in Israel. As a nation, they did not accept Jesus as their Messiah, but "God did not reject his people, whom he foreknew" (Romans 11:2). As a result of their rejection, "Israel has experienced a hardening in part until the full number of the Gentiles has come in, and in this way all Israel will be saved" (verses 25–26). Many believe that Israel continues to be God's timetable for the consummation of the ages.

The New Testament believers in the Early Church clearly understood that Satan and his demons were the instigators of evil in this world. The Western church is inclined to see the book of Esther as a battle only between good people and bad people. Such a deduction leaves a person to think that evil is purely the product of natural people living in a fallen world and operating under the permissive will of God, but that ignores the reality of Satan and his diabolical rule over the world. Satan interfered with God's plans in the Garden of Eden, and the battle continues all the way to the book of Revelation. The primary battle is still between the kingdom of

God and the kingdom of darkness, between the Spirit of truth and the father of lies, and between the Christ and the Antichrist.

In what ways does the book of Esther depict the spiritual battle between the forces of good and evil?

What are some of the ways that God preserved the Messianic bloodline?

How has God throughout history protected and preserved His people?

How would you summarize the battle between the kingdom of darkness and the kingdom of God?

What do you believe your role is in the kingdom of God?

But why was the Christ child sent into Egypt? The text makes this clear: He was to fulfill what the Lord had spoken by the prophet, "Out of Egypt have I called my son." From that point onward we see that the hope of salvation would be proclaimed to the whole world. . . . Even when they were engulfed in ungodliness, God signified that He intended to correct and amend both Babylon and Egypt. God wanted humanity to expect His bounteous gifts the world over. So He called from Babylon the wise men and sent to Egypt the holy family. . . . Keep in mind the long-suffering example of the mother of the Child, bearing all things nobly, knowing that such a fugitive life is consistent with the ordering of spiritual things. You are sharing the kind of labor Mary herself shared. So did the Magi. They both were willing to retire secretly in the humiliating role of fugitive.

John Chrysostom (AD 347–407)

Leader's Tips

The following are some guidelines for leaders to follow when using the VICTORY SERIES studies with a small group. Generally, the ideal size for a group is between 10 and 20 people, which is small enough for meaningful fellowship but large enough for dynamic group interaction. It is typically best to stop opening up the group to members after the second session and invite them to join the next study after the six weeks are complete.

Structuring Your Time Together

For best results, ensure that all participants have a copy of the book. They should be encouraged to read the material and consider the questions and applications on their own before the group session. If participants have to miss a meeting, they should keep abreast of the study on their own. The group session reinforces what they learned and offers the valuable perspectives of others. Learning best takes place in the context of committed relationships, so do more than just share answers. Take the time to care and share with one another. You might want to use the first week to distribute material and give everyone a chance to tell others who they are.

If you discussed just one topic a week, it would take several years to finish the VICTORY SERIES. If you did five a week, it is possible to complete the whole series in 48 weeks. All the books in the series were written with a six-week study in mind. However, each group is different and each will have to discover its own pace. If too many participants come unprepared, you may have to read, or at least summarize, the text before discussing the questions and applications.

It would be great if this series was used for a church staff or Bible study at work and could be done one topic at a time, five days a week. However, most study groups will likely be meeting weekly. It is best to start with a time of sharing and prayer for one another. Start with the text or Bible passage for each topic and move to the discussion questions and application. Take time at the end to summarize what has been covered, and dismiss in prayer.

Group Dynamics

Getting a group of people actively involved in discussing critical issues of the Christian life is very rewarding. Not only does group interaction help to create interest, stimulate thinking, and encourage effective learning, but it is also vital for building quality relationships within the group. Only as people begin to share their thoughts and feelings will they begin to build bonds of friendship and support.

It is important to set some guidelines at the beginning of the study, as follows:

- There are no wrong questions.
- Everyone should feel free to share his or her ideas without recrimination.
- Focus on the issues and not on personalities.
- Try not to dominate the discussions or let others do so.
- Personal issues shared in the group must remain in the group.
- Avoid gossiping about others in or outside the group.
- Side issues should be diverted to the end of the class for those who wish to linger and discuss them further.
- Above all, help each other grow in Christ.

Some may find it difficult to share with others, and that is okay. It takes time to develop trust in any group. A leader can create a more open and sharing atmosphere by being appropriately vulnerable himself or herself. A good leader doesn't have all the answers and doesn't need to for this study. Some questions raised are extremely difficult to answer and have been puzzled over for years by educated believers. We will never have all the answers to every question in this age, but that does not preclude discussion over eternal matters. Hopefully, it will cause some to dig deeper.

Leading the Group

The following tips can be helpful in making group interaction a positive learning opportunity for everyone:

- When a question or comment is raised that is off the subject, suggest that you will bring it up again at the end of the class if anyone is still interested.
- When someone talks too much, direct a few questions specifically to other people, making sure not to put any shy people on the spot. Talk privately with the "dominator" and ask for cooperation in helping to draw out the quieter group members.
- Hopefully the participants have already written their answers to the discussion questions and will share that when asked. If most haven't come prepared, give them some time to personally reflect on what has been written and the questions asked.
- If someone asks a question that you don't know how to answer, admit it and move on. If the question calls for insight about personal experience, invite group members to comment. If the question requires specialized knowledge, offer to look for an answer before the next session. (Make sure to follow up the next session.)
- When group members disagree with you or each other, remind them that it is possible to disagree without becoming disagreeable. To help clarify the issues while maintaining a climate of mutual acceptance, encourage those on opposite sides to restate what they have heard the other person(s) saying about the issue. Then invite each side to evaluate how accurately they feel their position was presented. Ask group members to identify as many points as possible related to the topic on which both sides agree, and then lead the group in examining

other Scriptures related to the topic, looking for common ground that they can all accept.

- Finally, urge group members to keep an open heart and mind and a willingness to continue loving one another while learning more about the topic at hand.

If the disagreement involves an issue on which your church has stated a position, be sure that stance is clearly and positively presented. This should be done not to squelch dissent but to ensure that there is no confusion over where your church stands.

Notes

Session One: God's Will

Chapter 2: Do All to the Glory of God

1. George Muller, quoted in Basil Miller, *George Muller: Man of Faith and Miracles: A Biography of One of the Greatest Prayer-Warriors of the Past Century* (Minneapolis, MN: Bethany House Publishers, 1972), p. 50.

Session Two: Faith Appraisal (Part 1)

1. Bob Benson, *Laughter In the Walls* (Nashville: Impact Books, 1996), pp. 22–23.

Chapter 3: Significance

1. Charles T. Studd (1860–1931), "Only One Life, 'Twill Soon Be Past."

Session Three: Faith Appraisal (Part 2)

1. Peggy Noonan, "You'd Cry Too if It Happened to You," *Forbes*, September 14, 1992.

Chapter 4: Security

1. "Historical Estimates of World Population," United States Census Bureau, 2013, accessed October 28, 2014, http://www.census.gov/population/international/data/worldpop/table_history.php.

Chapter 5: Peace

1. John Greenleaf Whittier, "Dear Lord and Father of Mankind," 1872, quoted at *The Cyber Hymnal*, accessed October 28, 2014, http://www.cyberhymnal.org/htm/d/e/dearlord.htm.

Victory Series Scope
and Sequence Overview

The VICTORY SERIES is composed of eight studies that create a comprehensive discipleship course. Each study builds on the previous one and provides six sessions of material. These can be used by an individual or in a small group setting. There are leader's tips at the back of each study for those leading a small group.

The following scope and sequence overview gives a brief summary of the content of each of the eight studies in the VICTORY SERIES. Some studies also include articles related to the content of that study.

The Victory Series

Study 1   God's Story for You: Discover the Person God Created You to Be

---

Session One: The Story of Creation
Session Two: The Story of the Fall
Session Three: The Story of Salvation
Session Four: The Story of God's Sanctification
Session Five: The Story of God's Transforming Power
Session Six: The Story of God

Study 2   Your New Identity: A Transforming Union With God

Session One: A New Life "in Christ"
Session Two: A New Understanding of God's Character
Session Three: A New Understanding of God's Nature
Session Four: A New Relationship With God
Session Five: A New Humanity
Session Six: A New Beginning

Study 3   Your Foundation in Christ: Live by the Power of the Spirit

---

Session One: Liberating Truth
Session Two: The Nature of Faith
Session Three: Living Boldly
Session Four: Godly Relationships
Session Five: Freedom of Forgiveness
Session Six: Living by the Spirit

Study 4   Renewing Your Mind: Become More Like Christ

Session One: Being Transformed
Session Two: Living Under Grace
Session Three: Overcoming Anger
Session Four: Overcoming Anxiety
Session Five: Overcoming Depression
Session Six: Overcoming Losses

Study 5   Growing in Christ: Deepen Your Relationship With Jesus

---

Session One: Spiritual Discernment
Session Two: Spiritual Gifts
Session Three: Growing Through Committed Relationships
Session Four: Overcoming Sexual Bondage
Session Five: Overcoming Chemical Addiction
Session Six: Suffering for Righteousness' Sake

Study 6   Your Life in Christ: Walk in Freedom by Faith

Session One: God's Will
Session Two: Faith Appraisal (Part 1)
Session Three: Faith Appraisal (Part 2)
Session Four: Spiritual Leadership
Session Five: Discipleship Counseling
Session Six: The Kingdom of God

Study 7   Your Authority in Christ: Overcome Strongholds in Your Life

Session One: The Origin of Evil
Session Two: Good and Evil Spirits
Session Three: Overcoming the Opposition
Session Four: Kingdom Sovereignty
Session Five: The Armor of God (Part 1)
Session Six: The Armor of God (Part 2)

Study 8   Your Ultimate Victory: Stand Strong in the Faith

Session One: The Battle for Our Minds
Session Two: The Lure of Knowledge and Power
Session Three: Overcoming Temptation
Session Four: Overcoming Accusation
Session Five: Overcoming Deception
Session Six: Degrees of Spiritual Vulnerability

Books and Resources

Dr. Neil T. Anderson

Core Material

Victory Over the Darkness with study guide, audiobook, and DVD. With over 1,300,000 copies in print, this core book explains who you are in Christ, how to walk by faith in the power of the Holy Spirit, how to be transformed by the renewing of your mind, how to experience emotional freedom, and how to relate to one another in Christ.

The Bondage Breaker with study guide, audiobook, and DVD. With over 1,300,000 copies in print, this book explains spiritual warfare, what our protection is, ways that we are vulnerable, and how we can live a liberated life in Christ.

Breaking Through to Spiritual Maturity. This curriculum teaches the basic message of Freedom in Christ Ministries.

Discipleship Counseling with DVD. This book combines the concepts of discipleship and counseling and teaches the practical integration of theology and psychology for helping Christians resolve their personal and spiritual conflicts through repentance and faith in God.

Steps to Freedom in Christ and interactive video. This discipleship counseling tool helps Christians resolve their personal and spiritual conflicts through genuine repentance and faith in God.

Restored. This book is an expansion of the *Steps to Freedom in Christ*, and offers more explanation and illustrations.

Walking in Freedom. This book is a 21-day devotional that we use for follow-up after leading someone through the Steps to Freedom.

Freedom in Christ is a discipleship course for Sunday school classes and small groups. The course comes with a teacher's guide, a student guide, and a DVD covering 12 lessons and the Steps to Freedom in Christ. This course is designed to enable new and stagnant believers to resolve personal and spiritual conflicts and be established alive and free in Christ.

The Bondage Breaker DVD Experience is also a discipleship course for Sunday school classes and small groups. It is similar to the one above, but the lessons are 15 minutes instead of 30 minutes.

The Daily Discipler. This practical systematic theology is a culmination of all of Dr. Anderson's books covering the major doctrines of the Christian faith and the problems Christians face. It is a five-day-per-week, one-year study that will thoroughly ground believers in their faith.

Specialized Books

The Bondage Breaker, the Next Step. This book has several testimonies of people finding their freedom from all kinds of problems, with commentary by Dr. Anderson. It is an important learning tool for encouragers.

Overcoming Addictive Behavior, with Mike Quarles. This book explores the path to addiction and how a Christian can overcome addictive behaviors.

Overcoming Depression, with Joanne Anderson. This book explores the nature of depression, which is a body, soul, and spirit problem and presents a wholistic answer for overcoming this "common cold" of mental illness.

Liberating Prayer. This book helps believers understand the confusion in their minds when it comes time to pray, and why listening in prayer may be more important than talking.

Daily in Christ, with Joanne Anderson. This popular daily devotional is also being used by thousands of Internet subscribers every day.

Who I Am in Christ. In 36 short chapters, this book describes who you are in Christ and how He meets your deepest needs.

Freedom from Addiction, with Mike and Julia Quarles. Using Mike's testimony, this book explains the nature of chemical addictions and how to overcome them in Christ.

One Day at a Time, with Mike and Julia Quarles. This devotional helps those who struggle with addictive behaviors and explains how to discover the grace of God on a daily basis.

Freedom from Fear, with Rich Miller. This book explains anxiety disorders and how to overcome them.

Setting Your Church Free, with Charles Mylander. This book offers guidelines and encouragement for resolving seemingly impossible corporate conflicts in the church and also provides leaders with a primary means for church growth—releasing the power of God in the church.

Setting Your Marriage Free, with Dr. Charles Mylander. This book explains God's divine plan for marriage and the steps that couples can take to resolve their difficulties.

Christ-Centered Therapy, with Dr. Terry and Julie Zuehlke. This is a textbook explaining the practical integration of theology and psychology for professional counselors.

Getting Anger Under Control, with Rich Miller. This book explains the basis for anger and how to control it.

Grace that Breaks the Chains, with Rich Miller and Paul Travis. This book explains legalism and how to overcome it.

Winning the Battle Within. This book shares God's standards for sexual conduct, the path to sexual addiction, and how to overcome sexual strongholds.

The Path to Reconciliation. God has given the church the ministry of reconciliation. This book explains what that is and how it can be accomplished.

Rough Road to Freedom. This is a book of Dr. Anderson's memoirs.

For more information, contact Freedom In Christ Ministries at the following:

Canada: freedominchrist@sasktel.net or www.ficm.ca

India: isactara@gmail.com

Switzerland: info@freiheitinchristus.ch or www.freiheitinchristus.ch

United Kingdom: info@ficm.org.uk or www.ficm.org.uk

United States: info@ficm.org or www.ficm.org

International: www.ficminternational.org

Dr. Anderson: www.discipleshipcounsel.com

Index

Notes

Notes

Notes

Notes

Notes

Notes

Notes

Notes

Notes

Notes

Dr. Neil T. Anderson was formerly the chairman of the Practical Theology Department at Talbot School of Theology. In 1989, he founded Freedom in Christ Ministries, which now has staff and offices in various countries around the world. He is currently on the Freedom in Christ Ministries International Board, which oversees this global ministry. For more information about Dr. Anderson and his ministry, visit his website at www.ficminternational.org.

Also From
Neil T. Anderson

This bestselling landmark book gives you practical, productive ways to discover who you are in Christ. When you realize the power of your true identity, you can shed the burdens of your past, stand against evil influences, and become the person Christ empowers you to be.

Victory Over the Darkness

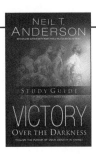

Great for small group or individual use, these thought-provoking personal reflection questions and applications for each chapter of *Victory Over the Darkness* will help readers grow in the strength and truth of their powerful identity in Jesus Christ.

Victory Over the Darkness Study Guide

BETHANYHOUSE

Stay up-to-date on your favorite books and authors with our free e-newsletters. Sign up today at bethanyhouse.com.

Find us on Facebook. facebook.com/BHPnonfiction

Follow us on Twitter. @bethany_house